Born in Reading in 1945, the author came to live by the sea on the south coast, when his father, a serving police officer, transferred there. Educated at the local grammar school, Peter was apprenticed as a printer, a trade in which he spent twenty years. The author has been a taxi driver for the last thirty years!

"WHERE TO, GUV?"

THE HILARIOUS MISADVENTURES OF A SEASIDE TAXI DRIVER

Dedication

In reversed chronological order:

To my long-suffering wife, who still doesn't know exactly what time I'll get home.

To my dad, who thankfully taught me to read at a very early age.

And, finally, to my grandfather, Max, who was quite a prolific author in the Victorian era.

Thanks, folks.

Peter Douglas

"WHERE TO, GUV?"

THE HILARIOUS MISADVENTURES OF A SEASIDE TAXI DRIVER

AUSTIN MACAULEY
PUBLISHERS LTD.

A CIP catalogue record for this title is available from the British Library.

Although essentially factual, certain names, places and dates have been changed to protect, well, practically everybody.

ISBN 978 184963 474 8

www.austinmacauley.com

First Published (2014)
Austin Macauley Publishers Ltd.
25 Canada Square
Canary Wharf
London
E14 5LB

Printed and bound in Great Britain

Contents

Preface

"Where to, Guv?" The meter starts, and off we go again.

For most people in the seventies, living in this small town, a ride in a taxi was a relatively rare event. Perhaps a quick dash to the railway station, as a substitute for one's car just when the damned thing won't start, the local casualty department, when young 'Erbert squashes his finger, a sad ride to the vets, an apprehensive visit to the dentist, and so on.

Taxis are readily available, day and night, to carry anyone, and most things, anywhere at any time to suit any customers' wishes. But most members of the wonderfully nutty public do not spare much thought for us, the drivers, perhaps imagining us to be a race of Troglodyte-like beings that emerge from our caves at a moment's notice to do their bidding, then retreat back into the gloom to await the next summons!

I have found from personal experience that people are as varied, interesting, and sometimes as downright infuriating as the loads and destinations themselves.

Advisor, friend, confidante, map-reader, childminder, shopper, removal man, and chauffeur, taxi drivers have been and always will be any or all these things to the people they try to serve. It is expected, and usually taken for granted. But – we try.

When recalling some of my most interesting exploits to a regular long-distance customer, he remarked that I ought to write a book. So I did. This is it. Read on!

Chapter 1
The Beginning

I nervously opened the office door and cautiously peered around the corner, coughing slightly as a thick fug of stale cigarette smoke billowed gently past me, as if trying to escape into the fresh air outside.

"Er…" I began, "I'm Pete, the new driver."

I was impatiently motioned inside by the man sitting at the desk in the corner. He tossed me a set of keys without looking up from the crackling radio in front of him, which squawked unintelligibly messages at him. I would eventually understand the patter, but it did seem to sound like a foreign language.

"Car's out in the yard," he barked. "Grey Lada. Check the oil and water, fill it up at the garage, PETROL mind, then I'll run through the job with you. Well, come on then!"

The four pairs of eyes that had swivelled curiously in my direction at my entrance, now re-swivelled back to their previous occupations of crosswords, making tea, of watching the ancient black and white TV perched precariously on an equally old bureau in the other dingy corner.

Clutching my precious keys, I rejoined the fresher air outside, and checked out my new steed. It was not impressive at first glance. True, it had once been grey, but neglect and rust in equal measures had taken their toll. The driver's seat sagged ominously, the odometer showed an incredible mileage when related to the year letter on the cracked number plate, and the tyres back up my first insight; evidence of some savage long-term abuse. I was new, so it was with some trepidation that I had to return to the office some fifteen minutes later to ask, amid much sniggering from the others, if some kind soul could please show me the bonnet release!

The engine, when examined, was almost buried under a thick protective layer of blackened oil, and various seemingly unrelated wires and cables, which had no obvious function, flopped here and there in glorious disarray. I closed the bonnet, and sat down in Mission Control, to await my first job, and could not help wondering just what I had let myself in for, as I, the rookie, mixed with the seasoned drivers. It was quiet now, and my mind drifted.

I had not set out in life with a burning ambition to do this job. A six-year apprenticeship in the printing trade, then a further fifteen years learning associated skills had been interesting enough, and satisfying in a hands-on way, leaving me with a lasting love and passion for most things mechanical, but the overtime had dwindled along with demand for traditional printing methods, so it was time to move on in a new direction.

My father had retired from the local police force, and found a job with a taxi firm to be his forte. He would regale me with hilarious tales of the people and places he came across, so it looked like an omen when a vacancy was advertised. I applied for my licence. The 'Hackney' licence and badge, and the accompanying compulsory test, consisted simply of a visit to the local DOE official, who grilled prospective candidates with a series of imaginary journeys and situations that the driver would be likely to encounter day to day, plus a medical, and the £20 fee.

The appointment was made and I was ushered in on the day. The examiner was well known for his tetchiness. He was due to retire soon and his boredom with the job was obvious.

"There are far too many taxis in this area already," he informed me. "I do not therefore intend to dish our licences to every Tom, Dick and [he glanced at my form] Peter that asks for one. By God I won't!" He emphasised every word with a thump of his fist on the desk. I took an involuntary step back. I knew he couldn't refuse my application, but he could make it difficult. "Right," he barked, "I'm a passenger in your car, heavily pregnant, in the town centre, and I want to get to the maternity hospital by the quickest possible route."

I eyed his advancing years with a cheeky retort on the tip of my tongue, but decided that discretion ruled, so just answered as accurately as I could. Hopefully, correctly.

He appeared satisfied, but disappointed. More routes followed, to and from all points of the compass, and by the end of an hour I was mentally exhausted. Judging by the frequency with which he surreptitiously looking at his watch, the interview was nearly over, his time was obviously pressing too.

"All right," he abruptly concluded, "your application will be presented at the next council meeting. Good day!" He strode from the room without another glance at me, so I wearily left also.

It took the best part of a fortnight to receive the council-approved licence, which included a plastic-encased ID photo. The likeness was appalling, but then so are most passports. That set me back a further £15, but I didn't care, I was accepted and on the road. In short a 'Cabbie!'

The first proper day at the job seemed to last forever, as it was clearly impossible to be as yet totally familiar with all the roads and back streets. It also seemed as if my boss took a fiendish delight in giving me the awkward addresses and passengers, especially the infamous ones that the other drivers knew well, and passed on to the new boy.

We were a private hire firm and as such could not pick up from the rank in town, instead relying on phone bookings.

The boss had a simple pay system; he paid for what was laughingly called maintenance, like tyres, servicing and so on. We would pay for fuel, plus so much a mile, so the shortest routes were essential. The rest of the monies earned was all ours. OK in theory, but I soon found out that going back to the office after each job soon used up fuel, unless journeys linked up, which was not often enough for our liking. The system of working was simple.

The first driver back got the next job out, but on slow days, with all drivers in the office, vast quantities of tea and coffee were quaffed, with marathon card games to pass the time eroding my earnings. I quickly found that my inane sense of humour, carefully nurtured over the years, plus an excellent memory for smutty jokes stood me in good stead with the others, and soon I was accepted. Too bad my memory did not always extend to addresses, but the variety of jobs and people was endless, as I was quick to realise.

Some passengers knew where they were, but were not too sure where they were going. Others were sure where they were going but, especially the more elderly who formed a large part of customers, not quite certain where they were speaking from!

Few other jobs that embrace the Great British Public can offer such amazing variety. NO two days were EVER alike, nor are they now, many years later. Eccentric people abound everywhere, and I do think we had more than our fair share.

The sheer plethora of journeys, characters and adventures I've encountered would fill many books, so welcome to the first!

Chapter 2
Dogs

"You don't mind dogs, do you driver?"

(After a relatively short time, the firm had enlarged enough to purchase, and trust me with, a Black Cab, the prestigious vehicle that alternated between the rank and the office, along with the coveted white plate, enabling me to pick up from anywhere. The cab's usage was shared among our drivers on a rota, each would drive for a week at a time, but for some reason it was not popular, so it was usually occupied by myself more than the others).

We were to hear this time and time again, and many journeys were undertaken, carrying pooches of all shapes and sizes belonging to the little old ladies that made up a large part of our clientele.

They went to the vets, from the vets, as a companion on shopping trips and so on. We even had one customer that required us to take the dog for a walk while she sat in the back of the car, watching the proceedings contentedly!

In a very short time, this particular lady became one of our firm favourites, and a call to her house was guaranteed to bring a smile to my face at any time of day.

Mrs Roberts, the doggie owner in question, would often go for a short ride to the outskirts of town to find a suitable stretch of woodlands in which to exercise her little dog 'Bagheera', obviously a Kipling fan.

It was then with some pleasure that I headed in her direction one sunny day, but the telephone message had me somewhat puzzled.

She said that she wanted to go to a dog show at Dappling village, a few miles distant, and I could not imagine 'Baggie' to be a typical show dog. Of a very definite non-descript type, he was composed mainly of Cairn terrier, with a good sprinkling of Peke! A thorough air of contented scruffiness completed his diminutive form.

Mrs Roberts was getting on in years, and a little forgetful at times, but the flat number given to me was not hers. I pulled up outside the building and went to ring the usual bell, but before I had time to complete the motion, a strident female voice boomed up to me from the basement area below.

"You there," she bawled, "are you my driver to the dog show?"

I peered with some trepidation over the railings, and my heart sank into my boots at what I saw. An extremely large woman stood there, glaring alternatively at me and at the biggest Great Dane I had ever seen in my life. It was trying its hardest to drag her bodily up the stairs to the pavement above, giving the impression of a contestant on the *Strongest Man in the World* competition on TV holding back a train!

"You don't mind dogs, do you?" she repeated, heaving on the lead. Her forearms must have benefitted greatly from this daily exercise! "He's no trouble once we get him into the cab."

With some trepidation I opened the door for them and watched in awe as the suspension sank a few inches under their combined weight!

"I assume you know the way?" she asked belligerently, as she fought to keep the dog still.

I replied, rather stiffly, "I would not be much of a taxi driver if I did not," but the irony was lost on her. The dog chose that precise moment to plonk his not inconsiderable bulk into her midriff, so depriving her momentarily of speech.

We set off, the dog balancing himself effortlessly on his dinner plate-sized feet, and his head just a few inches from the roof lining. He gazed with apparent interest out of the side windows. As the journey progressed, the woman thawed somewhat towards me.

"I can see that Pickwick likes you," she confided. (Another reader of classics, I mused).

I braked to avoid an errant cyclist, and Pickwick crashed gently into the bulkhead between us.

"He's a big softy really," she continued, "but he doesn't travel well, so I gave him half a tablet before we left."

I had a mental image of just what kind of mess this animal could make if he felt violently unwell, but quickly pushed it out of my mind!

Pickwick swayed gingerly from side to side as the cab negotiated a series of bends in the road, and it really seemed as if he was enjoying himself. Perhaps it was not going to be such a harrowing journey after all.

This idyllic notion sudden changed when he noticed the gap in the sliding glass partition behind me, separating the passengers' compartment from the driver's area. Without warning, he thrust his nose through and proceeded to give me a thorough and noisy sniffing. It was rather like sitting next to a large pair of bellows as he investigated the depths of my right ear. His exploratory tongue must have held the canine equivalent amount of water of a large sponge!

Obviously pleased with what he found there, he continued to lick my other ear, then neck with obvious pleasure, growling happily to himself.

I tried to shrink away from him by leaning forward, but his muscular neck and upper body was eminently suitable for considerably extension, allowing his slobbering lips and tongue to follow me as far forward as necessary to carry on his washing technique!

It was not until his whole hairy head was resting comfortably on my shoulder, that I realised that the worst had happened. The gap in the glass could not have been more than six inches at the most, but Pickwick's head was nearly twice that width, and wedged-shaped. By the time that the coarse bristles on his cheeks met mine, his head was well and truly stuck fast!

The situation did not seem to bother him much, but his mistress had quickly cottoned on to the situation.

"The show starts in one hour!" she shouted. "Stop the car and do something!" Her hysteria was transmitting itself to the dog, and now with rolling eyes he salivated freely in all directions as he tried to extricate himself from his predicament.

But this time I had entered a short stretch of dual carriageway so could not pull over for at least a mile or so. The previously happy growling had changed to an angry rumble, and I was in trouble.

The female sergeant major still harangued me, and I had to do something fast. Inspiration did not exactly flash, but a small glimmer was appearing in my mind. By sheer chance I had fitted a new battery to the cab the previous evening and the petroleum jelly I had used to coat the terminals was still in my pocket. Though only a small tin, it had to suffice.

I pulled over, put the brake on, and opened the tin.

Thickly coating the ears and neck of poor Pickwick, I placed both my hands over his muzzle and pushed hard. His natural reaction to having his tender hooter mauled was to back off, inching out of the gap, leaving the edges of the glass freely adorned with jelly and loose fur. His owner, of course, was furious, and immediately took his side against me.

"What's that silly man done to you?" she crooned, trying effectively to get rid of the sticky collar of fur on his head with a total inadequately-sized tissue.

I started off again, pointedly sliding the partition shut making a mental note to clean it properly at the next opportunity, then at last made it to Dappling and the village hall just in time for the show.

The woman hauled the dog out, carrying the usual mini suitcase full of the doggie cosmetics without which most owners would not be seen dead. She would not have too much trouble removing the harmless goo from his coat.

I was sorely tempted to stay and watch the show myself, but time was pressing. She was staying there overnight and I had to get back to the office.

The lady almost threw the fare at me, then vanished into the hall.

Just what state Pickwick was eventually paraded in, I never found out, for his mistress did not book the return journey with us.

I only hoped that the dog did not repeat his trick in some other man's cab on the way back!

Chapter 3
Horses

"It's 'er again, Mrs Plum in the gob!" the radio operator turned to me in exasperation. "She wants you to take her to someplace and I can't make out where the hell it is. Sounds like 'Eskit'. You speak to her. Blimey, I dunno, they want cab, but can I unnerstand 'em? Can I Ellerslike!"

I took the phone, and listened to the rather cultured voice on the line. Her real name was Lady S, and she was a 'titled personage', thanks largely to a very wealthy ex-husband and an even richer mother, who indulged her passion, horses, to the full. They frequently used our services to chauffeur the two of them around. The daughter could drive, but just why she never did was not discussed.

She repeated the destination and it was definitely 'Eskit'. What she mean, of course, as 'Ascot'. Not the racecourse, she hastened, but the showground. One of her horses was entered in the dressage event there on the next Saturday, and she wanted to see it in action. Would I take them?

Now, at this point you have to remember two very important points: firstly, the customer ALWAYS assumes that the driver ALWAYS knows not only the town in question, but also the quickest possible and therefore cheapest route, and secondly, no matter how far away the destination, no driver must ever admit that he does not know the area intimately! But, a job was a job, so the booking was made for two days' time. To complicate matters even further, Lady S stipulated that her mother and herself must travel to Ascot only on the motorway, as it was more direct, and they did not want to be unduly delayed.

In other words, they would, as usual, leave their departure to the last possible moment. Terrific! Not only did I not know where the showground was, but I hated motorways. The only good thing about this trip, apart from the priced remuneration, with the waiting time, chargeable at five pounds an hour, was the fact that my day out included a packed lunch, made by the mum's own fair hand. This shows thoughtfulness, and although I did not include horsey stuff in my list of hobbies, I found myself really looking forward to our day out in the country as I sped to their spacious sea front apartment.

Comfortably, though not ostentatiously furnished, it occupied a lovely position overlooking the beach, and I had often been asked to wait inside, while they got ready for shopping trips and the like. Hunting prints lined the hall, interspersed with large photos of favourite steeds from the past.

This day they met me at the door carrying a large wicker hamper, which hopefully was stuffed with goodies. (It would later turn out to be my undoing, a situation of which I was blissfully unaware.) The sun shone already and as I had glanced at my trusty map of the south-east region the previous evening, the route looked straightforward enough, so it was with a modicum of confidence that we set off.

They had long ago told their various drivers that rather than have the car radio on, they regarded it as a distraction to the art of conversation, they would prefer to be told something of the countryside as they journeyed around.

I'm certain that people fondly imagined that we unrolled a mental roller-map of the area as we drove along, including local facts, customs and gossip! I did my best until we drove out of our well-known towns and villages, but when our chatting turned into a discussion about breeding stock and pedigrees of horses, I used my standby method of amusing myself, namely – humming songs. Not audibly you understand, but comfortingly; and as they sat well back from me as I drive, I could also mime the words!

The motorway was not over busy, the cab hummed along nicely and so it was with minimum hassle that soon we were at

Ascot. Feeling father pleased, I then searched in vain for the venue. Signposts were there none, and glancing at the somewhat irritated expressions in my mirror, my humming increased in volume to placate myself. I couldn't be that far away, could I?

A roundabout eventually hove into view, upon which were two notices indicating the direction of the show. They pointed in two different ways, which doused my sudden elation like a bucket of water. I tossed an imaginary coil, and swung left, looking desperately for any sign of horse boxes or their accompanying Land Rovers.

Three miles further on, I was no nearer my goal.

My repertoire of sixties songs had given way to the classics, and I was sweating visibly! My annoyed passengers were totally agreed on the undeniable fact that I was lost.

I executed an urgent U-turn, sped back to that accursed roundabout, and took the alternative road. Fortunately, this proved correct and it was with a great sigh of relief that we swung into the 'Competitors' car park with a few minutes still remaining before the first event.

My mumbled excuses were received with cold expressions, and after telling me that they would return for lunch in about three hours, they vanished.

I leaned back weakly against the car and lit a badly needed cigarette. (That was another thing that they frowned upon on a trip out, but the last part of the two-hour drive HAD been stressful!)

I now had time to take stock of this gathering of equine enthusiasts. The central area was divided into two parts: the dressage ring and the jumping field. Around the periphery ran a double ring of shops, stalls and rows of tents, selling not only every conceivable kind of horsey paraphernalia, but also giving demonstrations of country crafts that promised to pleasantly occupy me until my stomach decided it was lunchtime.

The leather workers were particularly fascinating, with gleaming saddles being stitched, made-to-measure for any size bottom to be placed on any size horse! The prices reflected not only the best materials and workmanship put into the finished article, but also the deep pockets of the customers. The order books were filling up nicely even as I watched.

Not all the goods were out of my price range, however, and I bought a finely tooled leather belt for £4, which served me well for the next ten years.

The day continued sunny and warm, and although jodhpurs were the dress of the hour, with shiny boots as an optional accessory, ordinary chaps like me with ordinary jeans did not unduly stand out.

Individually wrapped and labelled 'Me', 'Mum' and 'Terry', the small parcels revealed themselves to be sandwiches of the finest ham, chicken and cheese. Three small identical flasks contained tea, then slices of Dundee cake, plain sponge fingers and a selection of fruit completed the feast in front of me.

It was about an hour before the appointed lunchtime, but I could just not wait. I took out one of the dainty china cups, sugared it, poured out half a flask full of their excellent Earl Grey tea and with a splash of milk, started on the food.

It was gorgeous, a smear of mustard on the ham, a dash of pickle on the chicken, custom-made to my preferences. I lay down on the short grass behind the car, and surrendered myself to the pleasant task ahead. Stretching my hand over the boot lid was no big effort, so soon the cake was beckoning. As I munched in culinary bliss I glanced at my watch. Five minutes, then they would be here. Time enough to clear away my debris, and prepare to serve their Hungrynesses. As I looked into the hamper, my blood froze. I could see the 'Me' packages, but that was all. I had eaten not only 'Mummies', but my own as well! Suddenly I was not comfortably full!

My brain switched into overdrive, and came up with the only solution possible; I had to try to purchase replacements, and fast.

I remembered passing a food stall in my meanderings, so that was my priority. I raced to the stall as fast as my stomach would allow, elbowed my way to the front of the queue, and blurted out that I had come for the sandwiches ordered earlier.

Of course the woman in charge had no idea what I was blathering on about, but sounding suitably indignant, I managed to get what I wanted, then hurtled back to the car, just in time to see Lady S, and her mother approaching from the opposite direction. Apparently, her horse had been placed second in both the dressage and the jumping, so she was more than pleased, her mood much improved from that of our arrival!

They showed no obvious surprise that I had dined already, and I handed round their re-wrapped fare with a smattering of nonchalance. So far, so good.

Her Ladyship tucked in hungrily, nattering enthusiastically about the prowess of her horses. Mummy got stuck in too, but with rather less gusto, I thought.

"Did you want to take the same route back?" I started, trying to give the impression that we really should be going.

"The country roads are very pretty, and I could point out some interesting places on the way."

They were both into the cake now, and seemed quite content. I relaxed a little, and confirmed that I had enjoyed the day out, especially the food provided.

We did return along the A-roads which proved to be a much better ride. It was five miles longer, but took only minutes more. So much for the supposed speed of motorways!

I carried the hamper indoors for them and put the proffered cheque into my wallet. As with the royals, Lady S never carried cash. As she turned to go back indoors, she exclaimed, "Do you know, Mummy, we really must have a word with the butcher. That chicken and ham was definitely not up to the usual standard!"

I managed to turn a relieved snigger into a cough, but as the door closed, I could have sworn that Mummy gave me a wink. Did they realise? I never found out, but they did not ask me again to take them to 'Eskit'!

Chapter 4
Girls

Strange how weather can affect our moods, emotions and even out marital status! A wet day, when it's blowing a gale, makes people grumpy. A warm, sunny spell makes people cheerful. The weather also governs, to a large extent, the number of potential passengers for the circulating cabbies. Mums and dads go shopping, for instance, then – down comes the rain. Caught out in a downpour, and usually some distance from the nearest bus stop, they hail a taxi, especially from the supermarket.

If the rain is too heavy, however, they don't go out at all! Conversely, if the day is too hot, the same result occurs. Ideally the day should consist of a light covering of snow, and an oncoming biting wind!

It was on such a lousy morning as I gazed expectantly at the passersby that one particular lady caught my eye. Tall and slim with nice legs, trotting briskly along the pavement.

Her raincoat had a plaid-patterned scarf around the collar, matching the lining of the coat, as it swirled around her knees in the wind.

On impulse, I waved and tooted as I passed, and was rewarded with a lovely smile and a wave in return. This small incident led me to actively look out for her, and I made a mental note of the time and place, reasoning that in my circuitous crossings of the town, we would be bound to meet again, and so it proved. But some days I saw her, some days not, and when we did meet it would always seem to be in a different place.

So where on earth did she work? It continued to be a bitterly cold winter, and I rehearsed what I would say to her when I had plucked up enough courage to stop and met her, face to face.

'Can I give you a lift, Miss?' – no she might be married.

'Can I give you a life somewhere?' – no too vague.

'Need a lift, I'm going your way?' – (wherever THAT was!) Mmm, that might do, I'll try it.

She seemed to have no set route, and so it could be any time of the day or evening when our paths crossed. Always the wave, and the dazzling smile. Short, curly hair and beautiful eyes too, I noticed. Then, at last, my chance came. There she was, the rain was lashing down, and I was free.

I pulled up alongside. "Hello," I began. "Er, un…" (What I mumbled next sounded like complete garbage, like Japanese spoken by a Frenchman!) I unscrambled my tongue and tied again, slowly. "Need a lift? I'm going your way." There done it!

"I'm only in that house about twenty yards up the road," she replied.

Well-spoken, I thought, perhaps a bit posh even, but at least I had made contact. She jumped in anyway. It was a start, AND I had found out where she lived.

In the days that followed, we ran into each other more frequently, and I found out that her name was Mary, and also that she cleaned peoples' houses, which explained her meanderings and why she never seemed to be in the same place twice!

It was nearing Christmas and one day she asked me for a price to take her to her parents' house, about fifteen miles distant on the afternoon of Christmas Eve. I knew that she worked now in a large wholesale fruit warehouse and was taking some to her folks. Her boss presented all the staff with these goodies, and as she lived on her own, the excess would be appreciated by them.

I met her at work, and after asking directions, loaded the boxes into the boot. I was momentarily alarmed by a man who hovered over us. Surely he was not coming too?

"That's my boss," she laughed, as he closed the door for her, so I sighed with relief as we set off.

I chatted more easily to her now and as the miles rolled swiftly by, it seemed as if I had known her all my life.

Soon we arrived, and I unloaded the cargo, then accepted the agreed fare. On impulse, with a rare show of bravery, I asked her for a Christmas kiss! She obliged, then again, and I returned to base several feet above the road's surface!

I had already asked her surname, and was mildly annoyed to find it was not listed in the local telephone book. either no phone, or unlisted. Plus, as yet, no address. Sherlock Holmes tactics were clearly called for.

By dint of careful observation, I discovered the bus stop at which she alighted to walk home. I waited for what seemed hours one day, then when she was seated next to me, asked EXACTLY where to drop her off.

"Number sixteen," she said with some surprise. "I thought you knew!"

Next, the flowers. Logical, but fraught with danger for a shy person like me. Oh, I bought them all right, and even walked up to the front door with them clutched nervously behind my back. The trouble was that unknown to me, a girl friend of hers had turned up at the same time.

She rang the bell, smiling to herself, then said, "Heidi," in answer to the entry-phone query.

Terrific, I thought, now what do I do? I decided that speed was the only answer, so when the door opened I thrust the bunch nervously at her, mumbled, "These are for you, see you later, bye."

On New Year's morning we met again, and tactfully not mentioning my faux pas (until much later in our relationship), she told me that she had to visit an elderly relative later that night, and see the New Year in with her.

Would she be able to get a cab home about one thirty? I told her that I would see to it, personally!

I had anticipated staying out until at least one o'clock, so no problem.

I met her at the appointed place, deep enough into a dark housing estate to put a protective arm around her shoulders as we walked to the car.

I had become so familiar with the layout of the town by now that I took the logical (to me) route back to her flat, but it was some time later that she confessed to me that, not only had she no idea where we were going, but she also wondered just what my intentions were, especially at that time of the morning!

Shortly afterwards, I took a passenger to the local night school, and had an hour or so to wait before picking them up, so I rang Mary's doorbell, explained the situation, and was invited inside for the first time. I accepted the offer of a cup of tea, and it seemed only natural to sit in an armchair with her sitting on the floor at my feet.

It was even more natural to reach out for each other in a long mutual hug. (I totally forgot the poor customer who got tired of waiting, so got another firm to take him home!)

The rocket I received the next day was well worthwhile, for within a very few weeks we became lovers, we found a much larger flat, then married three months later. Needless to say, Heidi came too Mary informed me at the reception that, upon my swift disappearance on her doorstep that embarrassing day, Heidi told her, "I think you'll be alright with him. He seems quite nice and sensible, for a TAXI DRIVER!"

Chapter 5
Wellies

A rather quirky, but quite likeable character was 'Green Wellies'. She was an upper class widow, a retired lady who lived in an apartment on the seafront. She sallied forth quite regularly to a 'club' in central London, to which the boss of our firm was always entrusted for the journey. Her conversation was rather limited, when we mere mortals did pick her up, to discussions about forthcoming shopping expeditions, and the general sloppiness of the local tradesmen.

She did sometimes reminisce about her late husband (apparently he was a Canadian Mountie, six foot six, and everyone called him 'Shortie'!)

We gathered that this reference was an in-family joke, because any further prompting on our part would just be met with a snigger.

She was also very mean in terms of tips, or rather lack of them, and gave the impression that generosity had NEVER been one of her attributes. She told our boss once that she missed her servants back in India, where she lived for a while after her husband died, poor them!

Winter and summer, she would always be seen dressed in a long, rather moth-eaten fur coat, and yes, calf-length green wellies, which fitted tightly around her ample legs!

(I did wonder if she sold the idea to the *Last of the Summer Wine* people!)

We always had to pull over to the kerb (not too close, mind), so that she had room enough to plant the size eight boots in the road before getting in or out. A drain cover was another definite thing to avoid, for fear of a slip.

So when the call to her flat came early one morning, I assumed wrongly, that she intended to go shopping in our town.

Settling THE coat around her, she said that her destination was a craft shop, not far away, to which she had previously taken a small, old-fashioned fire-screen to be repaired after an accident indoors.

On arrival she steamed into the shop, and emerged indignantly a few minutes later. "This is a shoddy job," she bitterly complained. "Fifteen pounds and it's really no better than when I took it in!"

I examined the poorly re-glued corners and cheaply re-glazed front. She was right, it was not a good job.

Now, as we all know, there are times when we have said things, then instantly regretted them. This was to be just such an occasion.

"I see your point," I said contemptuously. "I could do a better job than that!"

She looked at me thoughtfully for a moment. "Could you really, how splendid. How much would you charge?"

"Oh," I said, warming to my theme, "I could do that for a fiver, and have it back to you by tomorrow evening."

She agreed immediately and handed over the screen to me, then went inside.

I took it home, re-glued the mitred corners, used stainless pins for extra safety and put in an old piece of glass from a redundant picture frame.

I rang her bell late the next afternoon and was summoned upstairs into her, as yet unseen, living room. I barely stifled a gasp of disbelief, because the whole room, from dingy worn carpets, to sagging wardrobes, then on to threadbare settees, was a veritable shambles! Not the elegant room of a supposedly gentlewoman, but more an air of total neglect and decay.

She did, however, eagerly examine the screen, giving little murmurs of delight, gave me the five pounds, then ushered me out, telling me how grateful she was.

When I was again summoned to her flat the very next day, I feared that my very amateur repair had sprung apart during the night. I reluctantly ascended her staircase once again.

"I fear that I may have UNDERPAID you yesterday," she gushed. "Please accept another five pounds." Did I take it? Oh, yes!

Exactly the same thing happened the next day, and it appeared that her lowly screen had been ooed and aahed over by several of her cronies, and they had surprisingly agreed with me that she WAS mean! I was fast becoming famous for my antique repairing capabilities!

This might well have gone on indefinitely, had her favourite choice of footwear not been literally her ultimate downfall. While donning her well-loved boots one morning, she had tripped and fell over in the room, a fall from which she did not recover.

Her memory still lives on among the cabbies, however, as the eccentric lady who lived out her last days on the seafront, forever affectionately known as 'Green Wellies'.

As the regular customers became more familiar to me, so too did their little idiosyncrasies, the personal quirks that were to mark them forever in my memory. Such a strange person was 'Foggy Woggy', odd but likeable.

Her real name was Mrs Pulman, an elderly rather vague lady who lived in one of the better class of nursing homes that abounded in this area.

Of an outwardly meek and mild disposition, she would eagerly go out for her little shopping expeditions locally, and the usual fortnightly hairdressing appointment, but the BIG and very secret outing for her was reserved by phone to our office, specifically for every fourth Saturday.

The home staff thought it was just another ride out into the surrounding countryside for one of their favourite residents, but we the drivers knew quite differently. It was really to satisfy her never-to-be-mentioned passion: the roulette wheel!

There was a casino an hour's drive away along the coast, and there was never a hint of her destination when we picked her up, but the journeys were also conducted in the same manner, pulling up just around the corner of the home to await the furtive gambler.

Naturally well-dressed in tweeds, an Agatha Christie-type hat perched rakishly on her greying head, and the inevitable large, rather battered handbag, clutched tightly in her arms, she would climb on board.

As the casino did not at that time open all day, her evening would begin quite late, so invariably, almost as soon as the car had left the drive, she would doze off, only waking up when we approached the outskirts of the town, and we suspected also that she had a sherry or two after her dinner. (It was as if a personal radar warned her of the nearing establishment!)

The plan was, as soon as she had been ushered into the plush interior of the casino we would return in three hours, then drive her home.

This particular job was highly prized among the drivers, for the waiting time could not only be charged to the customer, but the period could be used to considerable advantage, like the beach, or a general walkabout, and as an ex-student of the local Arts College, I knew the back streets well, so did not take long to find a suitable non-metered parking space, so no time limit!

Sometimes she would be a little late in coming out, so this was an ideal opportunity to try to get a glimpse into the strange, hushed world of the croupiers, and the coloured chips that held such a fascination for the ardent fans of the wheel.

As a non-member, I could not go into the inner sanctum, where the action was, but even waiting inside the lobby was enough to get my pulse racing.

When she did emerge, there was never a hint of how well or how badly she had fared, while investing in the little tumbling ball!

She would get back into the car, and rather wearily survey the darkening world outside as we headed homewards.

When asked, she would only ever admit to winning or losing 'a few pennies', so the real outcome of her evening was only really known to herself.

Once out of the town's limits, our journey took us through the country roads, and along a long straight, known locally as 'The Marshes', skirted on both sides by fields and brooks, so as often as not, there were evening fogs drifting backwards and forwards across my path.

Mrs Pulham would be peering out, with failing vision at the night, and would always comment on the poor visibility when we reached this point.

"It's a bit misty-moisty tonight, isn't it?" she would quaveringly enquire. "A bit foggy-woggy."

Of course, the nickname stuck fast, and from that day on that WAS her name, but her eyesight definitely worsened rapidly.

This was proved conclusively when on a particularly dense 'pea-souper' evening's ride home, she asked me what, "Those men were doing standing at intervals along the roadside?"

(Quite how she could properly see the numbers on the green baize roulette table, I will never know, for the 'men' were TELEPHONE POLES!)

Again, no longer with us, she died a short while later in the comfortable surroundings that had been her home for many years.

Perhaps with an eyeshade, and under the bright overhead lights, she could see to gamble adequately. I just know that in the following years, a ride in poor visibility would be called a 'FOGGY-WOGGY'!

Chapter 6
Roundabouts

A certain smugness was apt to creep over me sometimes as I sat and waited for the next job. (Perhaps smug is too harsh, substitute readiness).

After all, armed with a full tank of diesel, a loaded sandwich box, flask of coffee, and a new packet of cigarettes, I could go anywhere within three hundred miles without being unduly bothered about where I was off to, or why. A sunny day, an empty road, and the world was my oyster. So was this particular day like that? Er – no, not exactly!

I was God knows how many miles up the M1, down to my last fag, almost out of fuel, and panicking slightly because I was nearly totally lost!

The day had started well enough, with a call from the office to collect some urgently needed carburettor spares from a specialist firm on the south coast and deliver them poste-haste to the Lola Racing Workshop at Milton Keynes. Simple enough, you may think? Read on, dear reader.

To the uninitiated, this wonderful town was merely a name, or a place to be hastily bypassed on the way to somewhere else, in other words a bit of a joke, so the first sight I had of it was a huge motorway sign that encouraged drivers to turn off to Milton Keynes North, South, East and West, or just the village of – yes, Milton Keynes! What a choice! Where to go?

I chose the village, simply because it might just contain that centre of local knowledge, THE PUB.

I stopped at the first one I came across, carried the parcel into the snug, and looked around me expectantly. The hum of conversation ceased at my entrance, and the landlord approached me from the end of the bar. I showed him the address hopefully, and sighed with relief as he nodded knowingly at the name on the label.

"You want the thirteenth roundabout," he said with a grin, "then turn left. I gather you're not from around here then?"

I shook my head wearily, and watch his grin broadened with delight at the prospect of yet another out of town driver getting lost on his home patch!

"Thirteenth, eh? Are you having me on?"

I hoped not, for in the last few miles up here, it had started to rain heavily, and my windscreen wipers had decided to sulk; they would not turn off!

"Oh no, matey," he chuckled, "there's a bloody great long line of 'em, from one end of town to the other, so make sure you start counting 'em from the first one you meet out of the pub 'ere, heading west!" He returned to tell the others at the far end of the bar, still laughing.

I bought cigarettes to aid my quest, and headed west. As he had said.

The rain was now settling down to a steady torrent, but – I had directions. The aid roundabouts when I approached them, were laid out in a dead straight line, with side roads coming off to the left and right of each junction, each road leading to many small self-contained industrial units, and a neat map put up at each crossroads. Very well laid out, this should be a doddle, I thought.

I heard, rather than saw the Lola Works from fifty yards distant, the roar of engines being far better than any signpost to one weaned on motorcycles!

INSIDE the factory unit, the noise was incredible, most of the men within having to wear ear-protectors. One of them signed for my parcel, and showed me where I could refill for the second leg of my journey. This was another package to Huntingdon, and the garage attendant suggested going back to Cambridge, then up towards the north, but a quick slurp from my ever-present flask, and a look at my rather dog-eared roadmap convinced me that a small road that headed almost directly east would link up nicely with the Huntingdon road.

I turned to leave the garage intending to follow this plan, when I had one of those infrequent strokes of luck that we could do with a lot more often!

A driver in the queue behind me had overheard our conversation, and told me that he was heading in the same direction himself, so would I like to follow him? He did not have to ask me twice!

Dusk was now falling fast, the rain still bucketed down (which was handy in one way, as I still could not turn the damned wipers off!) and I struggled to keep his rear lights in view, as he obviously knew the way far better than I, but it was faster than picking out the way myself.

Coincidentally, the second factory also handled racing cars, and the way that the other package was lovingly wrapped in bubble-wrap suggested that the contents were very fragile, perhaps computer components.

My guide stopped outside a likely-looking site, and I tooted my horn in thanks, as he sped off down a nearby muddy lane, and vanished into the deepening shadows, no doubt to a cozy little domicile.

I hefted the box inside the reception area and watched in amusement as a small puddle formed at my feet on the plush carpet in front of the desk.

The usual gum chewing receptionist peered at me over her designer specs, and asked me, incredulously, if I had really come this far on this sort of day in a taxi just to deliver a parcel. Several other girls stared equally bemused at me as they passed through, and it struck me that regular couriers must run the same verbal gauntlet many times a day in the course of their job!

It was by now almost totally dark, with just enough light to wrench out the fuse that fed the blasted wiper motor, then set out on the one hundred and fifty-odd mile journey back home to more familiar roads. Nearly all motorway, and quite boring, but fairly straightforward.

I had taken the opportunity to nip into the company toilet before departing; useful if you cannot easily stop for about three hours!

The system, when dropping off the cab, was to park it outside my boss's house, then ride the short distance home on my motorbike.

On this particular evening, however, I was about one hour late, and found my beloved BMW lying in a sad heap on the pavement, much battered! (Some spotty seventeen-year-old had borrowed Daddy's car, lost it on the bend before my parking place, and mangled the car, himself and my bike).

Witnesses were plentiful, thankfully, but the galling thing was not really the damage, though expensive to repair, but the fact that I had been there just one hour earlier this would not have happened.

Fortunately the driver, when patched up, went to the local constabulary and confessed, but it still took the best part of two months and two thousand pounds to put right!

It HAD been THAT sort of day, and I philosophically accepted it as such, but it just proved that in this game no two days are ever alike, and it NEVER pays to feel too smug!

Chapter 7
Greeks

"I would like you to take me to…" (Yes, I thought, somewhere away from all this, the Kasbah, the Riviera?) "Peckham," she continued, "to find a suitable college for my daughter."

The Greek lady who was speaking had been a good customer to the firm over the past few days, as we had been ferrying the two of them around the south of England in search of the future alma mater for the teenage Miss, who was very good looking, and had cheered up the drivers no end. Now it was my turn, and as I had not taken them anywhere yet, I looked forward to the outing.

The office had quoted £150.00 for the round trip to somewhere in London, plus a wait, then on to Southampton, plus another wait, then back home, which made a nice change to driving around town. There was only one snag: my hatred of driving in the city, so it was with some relief that I heard that the first destination was south of the Thames, less of a mystery to me than the city centre.

The mother asked me roughly how long the journey to Peckham would take, and after a quick calculation I said about two hours, depending on traffic. The two of them promptly rolled themselves up in their very expensive-looking sheepskin coats, and fell asleep.

This suited me very nicely as their English was not brilliant and our conversation had become a little stunted.

All went splendidly until we hit the A21, the main road into the outskirts of London. I needed a pee, and cursed that extra cup of tea an hour ago that had seemed a good idea then! I started looking for the motorists' friend, the garage. As I pulled into the forecourt, the cessation of forward motion woke up the two sleeping beauties in the back.

"Good morning," I joked. "Would you like some coffee? They sell it here, and I need some diesel." This, I thought, would kill three birds with one stone. As they disappeared inside, I put a few pounds worth of fuel in, then went inside to pay and fulfil my other and more urgent need.

The mum was shouting at the cashier, who was shouting more loudly back at her and other customers were queuing up to pay and staring at the floorshow in the shop!

I hurried to the gents, then rejoined the mayhem. As far as I could gather from the two participants in the action, two cups of coffee had been desired, and the correct amount paid into the machine on the wall, as per the instructions printed in large, clear lettering above it.

So far no problem, BUT the bad news was that, unknown to anyone except the cashier, the wretched machine only accepted tokens to the value of the drinks, NOT coins, and these were only available from – yes, the wretched man behind the desk!

This was bad enough, but you also had to use a kind of cassette of pre-wrapped coffee, and two such packs, together with several coins, had well and truly jammed the machine up solid. The man was most definitely not amused, so it seemed an excellent idea on my part to pay for my fuel, then leave smartly, which I did, ushering my two charges outside.

They had got their money back, but to my horror as they reached the door, mum, still clutching her empty plastic cup, turned back and said, "How much for the cups, please?"

"They're free, madam," he sighed heavily. "Please take them with my compliments!"

I offered them some proper coffee from my ever-ready flask, and peace was temporarily restored.

We found Peckham College without further mishap, and I even found a parking space when they had gone in, so I finished the flask, read the paper from cover to cover, had a cigarette and a recce. Mission to the college loo. All this took just over an hour, and after checking with the receptionist on the desk, I found that not only were the ladies over an hour early, but their tour of the facilities would take another hour and a half. Terrific!

Traffic wardens being unusually absent, I dozed off, only to be awoken by a frantic tapping on my window. The daughter wanted to phone ahead to the next college, to rearrange the timetable at the next educational expedition in Southampton, as they were now running late, and, of course, she had no change.

The receptionist, bless her cotton socks, had suggested an alternative at Farnham, near Guildford, which she thought would be nearer, time wise, and I had to agree this was preferable. They did too, given the time remaining. So I asked the by now bemused desk girl the best way.

"Up to the Elephant, get on the A3, leads you straight through to Guildford, love."

This sounded good to me, so we set off again, after a trip to the neighbouring sweetshop for a huge bag of assorted chocolate, through which they munched, then again fell asleep until the outskirts of Guildford about an hour later.

"Almost there," I said encouragingly, "a few more miles."

Into Farnham, I pulled up next to a Post Office van to check. His answer was half-expected: "You're miles away, mate!" My optimism was receding fast. I wish I had a pound for every time I'd heard that sentence in my job. "Go back to the direction Winchester sign," he advised, "then come back into Farnham from the other end. The college is signposted as you come in."

Again, when I'd done this, I struck lucky parking wise. The college was directly opposite Safeway's car park. After asking, this time, how long they would likely to be inside, I toddled off round the town for the next two hours. The primary objects being to satisfy my thirst, one way or another, and perhaps to take in couple of bookshops, of which there were apparently hundreds and of which I'm passionately fond.

Could I find one? Could I heck! But watering holes, no problem! By now it was getting dark, getting colder and raining heavily. So back to the comparative warmth of the car and an apple; the only scrap of food I had left after eating my (also always-present) sandwiches during my wanderings around the town.

To my relief, it WAS two hours later that they reappeared, looking very tired, and I did not argue when they asked me to take them home again. THEY had supped rather well inside the college restaurant (why didn't I think of that?), so they soon nodded off in the cozy heat of my taxi, leaving me to more easily navigate the route home, which took until six o'clock.

They asked to be dropped at McDonalds, and paid me the revised fare of £30.00 less, but with a good tip thrown in for good measure.

I headed for the creature comforts of home myself, and as I lay luxuriously in a hot bath shortly afterwards, I reflected on the events of the day. The ladies had told me at the finish of today's ride that they had decided to go to Southampton anyway, so this would probably be with another driver. I wondered if he would have such an interesting day. I doubted it very much, unless they stopped off for coffee!

Chapter 8
Theatricals

I love characters, you know, the people that stand out from the rest, and the chance to link such a person with potentially stimulating ride out of the area, to alleviate the tedious daily grind of driving around town, coupled with my widening knowledge of the countryside around our base, was most welcome. Even so, when a call came in to take a 'Shakespearian actor' from a hotel on the seafront to a workshop out in the country where he was due to make a sound recording at the studio of the Talking Books organisation, I had to look up the village in question in the map book.

I could not help but have a mental image of a tall, distinguished-looking gentleman, wearing the trademark long cloak and top hat. When I picked him up the next morning, he was exactly so, complete with white gloves, and shiny black patent boots, spat-covered naturally!

Originally a one-off, these trips were extended to a week, taking him out at nine, and returning to pick him up at four, leaving the rest of the day for the usual jobs that comprised our working day.

He said that he preferred the same driver every day, so my week was booked accordingly.

The first journey, both out and back was fairly uneventful conversationally; which was not really surprising as new passengers did not usually supply me with their life stories upon our first meeting, but as the week progressed, he became more talkative, and regaled me with many anecdotes of his life in and around 'the theatre'.

He had obviously travelled quite widely and his knowledge of the early lives of many music halls stars who went on to relative fame, then stardom, was extensive; his advancing years doing nothing to diminish his excellent memory for facts and figures.

He seemed interested, too, in my humble comings and goings in my trade, so the days flew by until it was the last day's ride out for him.

On the final ride home, he provided me with a story that still makes me chuckle many years later, and retells better every time!

"Do you mind, dear boy [I mentally winced at the familiarism, which I assume actors bestowed on their companions] if I tell you a rather risqué tale?" He had gathered by now that I had a broad sense of humour, but as I had also gathered that his sexual preferences were leaning towards the male side, I wondered if his idea of a rude joke was the same as mine!

"Nowadays," he began, settling himself on the edge of his seat and speaking conspiratorially close to my ear, "theatres are used for a great many more things than plays. Concerts, meetings and," he shuddered visibly, "bingo must run alongside we players on order for it to survive." His voice trailed off, as if remembering the awful vision of alternatives to the only true use of the boards.

"We were due to open in Darlington," he returned to the narrative, "in mid-winter at a little theatre that was really on its last financial legs, and due to close inside a month, so the audiences were not exactly expected to fill the place to overflowing."

His rich baritone voice was taking on enthusiasm now, and it did not take too much imagination on my part to visualise his filling of the auditorium with the sound of the Bard's finest lines!

"What we did not know," he enthused, "was that we were due to start off the performance that evening, immediately following the afternoon's private party with strip shows, and the timing was extremely tight."

I began to chuckle as the mental images began to form, but I could not have foreseen the outcome to the story, as he warmed to his theme.

"It was sheer chaos, dear boy. The girls in their show were only just changing to go as we were trying to change to go on, and the scenery shifters threatened a walk-out and to leave us to do it all ourselves."

Then, he had a brainwave, a real humdinger of an idea. He went to the girls' changing room, which must have taken some considerable courage, and somehow persuaded one of the strippers to give the not immediately active members of the company (he paused to mentally compose the sentence), a 'quick private viewing' to expedite the smooth changeover of backdrops etc.

This, he rightly assumed, would no doubt cheer up the more masculine amongst them, giving those with no interest in the proceedings time to sort out the mess backstage.

She apparently readily agreed, and came to the curtained-off area front stage to briefly disrobe again.

This went down very well as he has suspected, the intended mutiny was forgotten and peace was restored. The said lady received probably a bigger cheer than on her first performance!

The seating was rearranged for the play, the scenery was set out a planned, and the actor was well pleased with himself, so much so that he went backstage to the lady's dressing room once more to thank her personally.

I heard furtive swallowing noises, and I suspected that he must have had a swig from his ever-present hip flask, for the next thing that he told me had even me gasping at his boldness.

A sudden naughty thought had apparently struck him as he turned to leave her room.

"You're obviously no youngster, madam, if you don't mind an elderly man saying so," was his new opening gambit. "Can you tell me how it is that you keep your er – um…" he glanced meaningfully towards her pubic area. "How it is…" He was going to finish the sentence if it killed him. "That your thingy is in such – er – good condition?"

I could only imagine the reply.

Far from infuriating the good lady, this undeniably cheeky and very, very personal question seemed to greatly amuse her. "No one," she chuckled, "ever has previously ever asked it. Well, confidentially, dear boy," she cooed (perhaps THAT was where he got the dreaded phrase from) bending down so that she could whisper conspirationally in his ear, "we use WIGS for other things than putting on our HEADS!"

He leaned back into this seat as if the retelling of the tale had been painful, but I thought it was priceless, and mentally assigned it to a chapter of my future book.

We had reached his hotel now, which was just as well for I had trouble concentrating on the road through my tears, but it was with real regret that I bade him farewell on this, his final, day.

I saw him just the one time more, when I took him to the station the next morning. We never met again, and it had been a real pleasure riding with probably one of the last original and traditional thespians of our day, but coincidentally the very next week I picked up a partially sighted man, who spoke in glowing terms of the selection of tapes that the Talking Book Society had sent him from which to choose his preferences.

"I am particularly taken," he said, "by the Shakespearian-sounding gentleman, whose voice really makes the spoken stories come alive!"

I bet that there was ONE story he didn't dare put on tape for distribution!

Chapter 9
Monasteries

Mundane everyday journeys were bread and butter to us, of course, and to catalogue each one would fill several notebooks, so only the ones that really stood out in my memory have been committed to pen and paper.

One such episode was the artist, her paintings and her husband. She called our office one day to book an outing to a little village some miles out of town, in order to take some paintings for sale to a buyer who collected watercolours of the surrounding countryside. I liked to mentally picture an image of these people, and the stereotyped artist was not to let me down.

She answered my knock to her door wearing a long, painty smock, no shoes, and looked suitably vague as befits an artistic temperament. She gazed at me for several seconds before the penny dropped. Recognition of just who would dare to disturb her doings, was confirmed by looking past me to the cab outside!

She gestured equally vaguely at bundles of wrapped frames strewn haphazardly on the floor, and told me to load them into the car, adding that she would join me as soon as she had changed into 'street clothes'.

She emerged a surprisingly short time later, but the only difference I could see, was that she had put some shoes on and a coat over her smock!

As usual, to a new driver, she was not over-communicative, but as the miles unwound, I casually inserted into the faltering conversation the fact that I had fairly recently taught myself the rudiments of watercolour painting, and would very much appreciate some guidance. She became more talkative, and so the ride became all the more enjoyable to us both.

The main reason for selling her paintings, she said, was to finance the purchase of more materials to continue the ongoing renovation of her cottage, into which her husband and herself had recently moved, after their marriage of just a few months. I had not taken much notice of the tall man who had said goodbye to her at the doorstep, other than he was probably quite a bit older than she, and had dressed just as scruffily as herself.

Soon we arrived at the rambling manor house where the sale was due to take place, and I helped her to unload the pictures into the salesroom.

She gave me a five pound note to buy some lunch, which was a very nice gesture, I thought, and told me to return in a couple of hours to take her back home.

So far, so good, I thought, and hurried off to the nearest pub to comply with her wishes!

Timekeeping in the taxi business is everything, so I got back to the manor early, hoping to have a quick getaway, and was ushered inside, by I presume the owner, who said they would not be long finalising their business, and would I like to wait inside?

I realised then that she was not the only person selling paintings that day, for about a dozen people filed past me on their way out, carrying bundles under their arms, all very smartly dressed; many in proper tweeds, some stuffing cheque books back into their pockets, and looking very pleased with themselves.

My artist finally appeared, apologising for the delay, and off we drove. She had sold all her paintings, she told me, and was obviously in a happy, expansive mood.

The cottage, she went on, was proving to be much more expensive to renovate than she had been led to believe by previous owners, and today's sale would just about bring in enough to pay for the finishing touches to the master bedroom, which, she said proudly, contained a genuine antique French double bed!

I said that I doubted if there were many of those in the south of England, and asked her, rather cheekily, if there was any connection between this bed and the two of them, as she did not sound like she was of French extraction. She laughed, and related to me what she insisted was the true story of how they had come to be together.

Her husband, she said, had originally been a monk for over twenty years in a small monastery in a remote area of France. His duties were minor, even after twenty years of service, and he had only just 'graduated' to the tending of the past Abbot's graveyard. Though an undemanding man, and well used to the frugalities of monastic life, it nevertheless occurred to him one day that, unless he made Abbot soon, he would probably wind up in the same graveyard himself! This called for some immediate action on his part.

Without further ado, he left the Brotherhood and moved, penniless, to Paris. Some of the crafts he had learned over the years must have come in useful, for within a year he had rented and furnished his own apartment and taught woodcraft and carpentry.

The bed was taken as payment for a course in woodcarving that he had given to the son of an antique dealer.

His wife, the artist, had met him as a student and had fallen in love with him, eventually persuading him to come to England and then they had married.

They had found their ideal future home in the cottage at which I had found them, and had lived there happily ever since.

To my ever enquiring mind, this posed the inevitable question, and before I had the courage to ask her, she beat me to it. (Yes, the honeymoon!)

She laughed again, as if relishing my curiosity about them. The ex-monk had realised his ignorance of things sexual, and realising that his future wife may have certain needs, had thoughtfully engaged the services of an expert French prostitute!

The story of his further education was duly confessed to his wife-to-be, who, far from being devastated, found the tuition both amusing and instructional. Proving to be both an excellent pupil AND teacher, she said, he had made the honeymoon a roaring success, and the lessons were still continuing to this day. (I wondered if certificates were awarded, but did NOT ask her!)

The conversation turned to other topics, and the ride home passed very quickly. Too quickly, for I was dying to hear other anecdotes from this fascinating lady, but as always with interesting passengers, all too soon we had arrived back at journey's end, the cottage.

She paid me well, and I believe that a pleasant chat goes down very pleasantly with the average companion on a day out, but also I like to think that perhaps she had not told TOO many other people about the amorous monk and his artist lady. After all, taxi drivers are like doctors, the information is confidential, until I wrote this book!

I did hear several years later that they had moved again to a larger, even older place somewhere out in the country. Her paintings were becoming sought after and collectable, and yes I did buy one of her early works, and he was selling good quality woodcarvings to the upper end of the market.

Good luck to them, genuinely nice people, and I hope THE BED survived the move and is still serving them well!

Chapter 10
Photographers

It was 6am, dark, raining heavily, and damn cold, as I headed out to pick up a young man to take to Gatwick Airport. I hoped he was ready for me.

I found his flat easily enough, and loaded several trunks and suitcases into the boot, opened his door for him, then set off up the road. Five minutes into our journey, his mobile phone warbled. It was his wife; gently reminding him that if he wanted to catch his flight, he may need his passport, which was on the kitchen table! We turned around, picked up the needed item, then set off again, having lost time that we could not afford, for my passenger, along with most holidaymakers, had left himself the barest minimum spare time before checking in, so now I had to hurry to make it up.

He asked politely if he could smoke in an obviously French accent, and as I accepted one of his Gauloises, I remarked that obviously his strip abroad was not a short one, judging by the amount of luggage he was taking, and asked if he was off to somewhere nice.

He told me that the trunks contained camera equipment, and that he was booked into a desert island to do a photo shoot with the Jagger family!

At this time of the morning, I was usually on autopilot, but I did listen with at least half an ear, as he went on to talk about some of the stars that he had photographed.

"I've just finished a calendar," he said proudly, "with some of the best-known sports personalities in the world!"

Yeah, yeah, pull the other one, I thought.

"Chris Eubank, 'e was a gentleman. The rugby stars can be difficult 'Enry Cooper was charming. Footballers are a bit nervous having me posing them, but the one man 'oo really 'as a mind of 'is own is Carl Fogarty."

I snapped into fully awake mode, and looked at him incredulously. "Carl Fogarty!" I croaked. "Really, THE Carl Fogarty?"

Now my particular penchant, sports wise, was motorcycle racing, specifically World Superbikes in which 'Foggy' was the current champion, and my hero. I decided to test him out, so I asked him several questions, which someone who had met the great man would know.

"Which bike did he ride?" Ducati: one right.

"Any outstanding features?" Tall, with piercing blue eyes: two right.

"Wife's name?" Michaela: third answer right.

I think this guy is genuine.

"The photos were to be used for the forthcoming autobiography," he said.

I listened, fascinated, as he told me of the studio sessions with Carl posing in his racing leathers, sitting on his beloved Ducati.

Carl was a brilliant man to work with, he said, and would listen intently to any instructions given to him, but did not suffer fools gladly, and knew his own mind. He could tell what poses would work, and which would not, so most of the shots would be compromises, and the result were superb. I could imagine from the public image of him, that you did NOT push him around, verbally or otherwise!

The journey passed very pleasantly, and as we neared Gatwick, the photographer remarked that although Carl had OK'd the portfolio for the book and the content and sequence of the photos had been chosen, he had obviously used several rolls of film too many, in order to select the best from them all, so he had 'a few dozen' spare. Would I like a couple?

Would I! WOULD I! This could really make my day, or even my week!

I dropped him off at the appropriate terminal, and arranged to pick him up in a few weeks' time and I would collect the prints then (hopefully).

The other drivers were very sceptical when I told them my highly unlikely tale, but as I again met the Frenchman a week later, my optimism was running high. He was full of his shoot on the island, and told me some surprising idiosyncrasies of the Jagger family, especially Mick; but no, I can't write them here, they are confidences between us, so there!

As we unloaded the photographic paraphernalia again, and stowed it in his basement flat, he proudly showed me the darkroom, with the developing and printing equipment. He then sorted me out two handsome eight by twelve prints of 'the man', which I subsequently had framed, and hung them prominently on my wall at home, but not before running off several black and white copies for the disbelieving, but equally enthusiastic drivers at work.

His next assignment, he said as he cut short my effusive thanks, was to be a one-man exhibition in London and other cities, and he is as well-known in the world of fashion as he is sports wise. I hope he is recognised for his abilities, for in my humble opinion, he has got what it takes to go far.

No photos, however, will take a bigger pride of place than the two 'Foggies' that greet my visitors as they open my front door, taken by the unassuming, but forgetful French photographer!

Chapter 11
Trees

A student of nature and a lover of flora in general, trees and me get on! I've sat in them as a youngster, smoking an underage fag, tried to (unsuccessfully) paint a decent representation of foliage in watercolours and even planted them in my garden at home, under which shade I would quaff a cold beer at the end of a stressful day, but I had a real good reason one day in summer to take genuine dislike to a particular specimen of oak tree.

Two very elderly ladies had booked me to take them about twenty miles out of town, to a rambling old house, which was easily found, they said, when we got to the village, and then I was to leave them there until the next day when they would have bought everything that their little hearts desired at a typical country house auction! Easy enough, in theory.

Setting off is usually the best part of any journey, next to the finding of the destination, then the dropping off of the passenger to return alone, all the better to enjoy the ride back at leisure, unless the paying occupants of my car were particularly interesting to talk with, and these two WERE.

They were collectors: china, books, dolls and small furniture items. Where on earth they put it all and whether they sold it on at a profit, I do not know, but their cottage was small, and certainly not originally designed for hoarding!

They eagerly scanned the catalogue on the way there, and discussed possible under-pricing, overpricing, and hopefully getting to the sale early enough to peruse possible bargains before they were spotted by the greedy dealers. These sales, they observed, were full of such scoundrels, who bought up the best prices at rock bottom prices, and it would not come as a surprise to them if the whole sale was rigged in the dealers' favour!

The village was easy to find; the house was certainly not. Its name was on the heading of the catalogue, but no road or street was mentioned, and if it were not for an errant postman on his way home at the end of his early shift, we would not have found it that day, let alone early.

The house lay at the very end of a steep Y-shaped gravelled drive, heavily overgrown on all sides by overhanging trees, which gave a general air of neglect to the whole place, born out by the gloomy old stone manor at the end of the sloping approach.

A huge, ancient oak tree grew in the very centre of the fork of the Y-shape, and I had to drive carefully around the massive trunk to reach, or even see the massive metal-studded entrance doors to drop the ladies off.

The ladies got out, paid me and arranged a pick-up time for the morrow, apparently staying at a local inn in the village overnight.

I wished them good bargain-hunting, and got back behind the wheel. As I slowly reversed out to turn around, one of them reappeared from the entrance and shouted something at me.

Stupidly (very, very stupidly), instead of stopping, I leaned out of the window, to more clearly hear her, at the same time pressing the brake pedal, and pressing instead on the accelerator! Can you picture this? Read on! Exactly what happened next is indelibly, permanently, etched on my memory.

There was a loud crunching noise from the back of the car as backwards motion abruptly ceased, followed by the tinkling sounds of small pieces of metal hitting the ground, and gentle clouds of dust floated down around me from the roof lining. Oh, yes, I had backed into that blasted oak tree! I sat there stunned, not physically, but by my own total carelessness.

The lady, not waiting to hear the answer to her shout, and oblivious to my own predicament, had gone back inside to her beloved sale, and it was not until I heard another, louder male voice approaching, that I returned to reality. The man had run out from the rear of the house and stood by my door, breathing heavily.

"I say," he said anxiously, "are you alright? I heard the bang from the garden. Is the car badly damaged?"

I gazed at him sadly and nodded. "I expect so, I haven't the heart to have a look yet," I told him resignedly. Brushing the internal debris from my trousers, I got out and followed him to the rear of the car, which did seem awfully close to that accursed tree. It WAS pretty badly re-modelled! The bumper was not outer bark-shaped, sort of wrap-around, and the remains of the rear lights lay on the drive, one reversing light irritatingly still alight! The boot opened, just, but then maddingly would not quite shut. Brilliant!

The owner of the house, for as such he had introduced himself, went back into the garden, reappeared a few minutes later with a length of plastic-covered wire, and between the two of us wired the boot securely shut. The car was driveable, so I pulled forward, turned around, and prepared to leave the scene of the disaster.

The man's departing words will stay with me forever. "You should have come tomorrow," he said, "so many people have done that, we're sawing it down!"

I looked deep into his eyes, expecting to see a twinkle, but no, he was serious! I sighed heavily, then drove away.

The car WAS repaired, and I stayed with it, but trees! I hate large oaks!

Chapter 12
Films

Most cats love me. Most dogs tolerate me. Children either take to me, or they don't. There does not seem to be any halfway stage.

One child who definitely took a shine to me right from the very beginning, was Michael, whose name I have changed. He was a spina bifida victim of about eight years old, and I ferried him to and from a specialist boarding school once a week on Monday, then home again on Friday.

He almost lived in a special wheelchair, which kept him bolt upright during the day, although he could sleep in a normal bed, but had to be lifted in and out for calls of nature, and for daily massage sessions, as he was limp and helpless out of his supporting frame.

In the chair, he was a nightmare of mobility, changing directions quicker than I could on my two feet, and the word 'fear' was not to be found in his vocabulary.

Well-strapped into the rear of my cab, speed was his passion, and a bumpy, pot-holed road was a bonus to him, provoking shrieks of delight from the wildly rocking wheelchair.

Although not exactly imprisoned at home, for he had fantastically dedicated parents, and two 'ordinary' brothers who adored him, life was obviously not easy for him.

My own son had a ninth birthday party coming up, and I asked Michael's folks if he would like to come too. I would pick him up and return him at a decent time afterwards. They readily agreed, and the young lad was very enthusiastic, and talked about nothing else in the previous week's journeys.

I briefed my son and his friends, which was a little tricky, as he had never met anyone who was physically handicapped, not to regard Michael as being 'different'. He was to be accepted, and to be helped if needed to join in the games, which worked brilliantly. He was having a ball. So far!

The succession of goodies were consumed in astonishing quantities, squash was quaffed by the gallon, and the usual games went swimmingly, judging by the gales of childish laughter coming from the games/dining room.

Then came the coup de grâce. A friendly video shop owner had reserved for me a new Disney cartoon on the first day of release. The stage was set, the lights dimmed, and the room was expectantly hushed.

The credit rolled, the opening music blared, and the film began. The whole room gasped as the title came up; not *The Beauty and the Beast*, as eagerly anticipated, but *Sex Kittens of Europe*! OOPS!

Even the very first frames were quite graphic, so the film was soon stopped!

The proper film was hastily sent for and shown, but for years afterwards the birthday party film show was written into the legends of the neighbourhood!

Michael never let on to his father exactly what had happened, but I suspect that several fathers that had been present on the night may have paid a visit to the video shop later to see the rest of the first film!

Michael had a shortened life, for he died a few years later while out in the countryside that he loved, picking strawberries with his family, but many was the time on the way to and from school that he would remind me of 'the film', with his usual trademark shrieks of laughter!

****

On occasion, when precious spare time permitted, and a local photographer was too busy to manage everything himself, I would help him out by taking my other hobby paraphernalia along – cameras and flashgun – doing weddings, christenings, even the rare burial coverage, and these outings provided plenty of experience and amusement for me, as well as a small fee for attending.

Most went very well, a few ended in family arguments and one prospective bridegroom actually stormed off, never to be seen again!

Most guests were co-operative, even when told where to stand or sit, and many a glass of sherry or champagne was eagerly accepted at the end of a long session, before rushing back to the studio to examine the prints.

Now, bear in mind the era is the sixties, and the norm was black and white film; colour was a lot extra for developing and printing, and was sent away for processing, so delaying the production of the wedding album for perhaps a week. Normal prints were delivered the next day, as a rule.

Time did not normally permit me to join in at a sit-down reception, so the odd sandwich was all I normally went with.

Never, never forget to take enough film with you, and always, always have a spare camera body pre-loaded for speedy changeover, for there will come a time when you will need that extra, quick shot.

This was hammered into me by my professional photographer tutor, and I never did. Well, only once, and again a small boy was part and parcel of the adventure.

The wedding was at a local country church, really more like a large wooden hut in the middle of a mown field, and I arrived in good time to set up my equipment. The sky was blue, the day was fine, and I had high hopes of a nice time to be had by everybody present. I had been briefed on the family members, who were a little unusual, even in my limited experience.

The bridesmaid party consisted of three pairs of sisters, who naturally wanted plenty of pictures of themselves in several permutations of groups. Also included in the posing process was a single pageboy, George, aged about eight, who at the time was very smartly dressed and well-behaved.

The bridesmaids, all in their late teens, wore dresses of pastel tints, no two being alike, and with the suited pageboy in their midst looked fabulous.

The bride arrived with her father, and posed very prettily for her own photos. This can take time, arranging the train behind her etc., but at last she stood at the church door, arm in arm with her dad and the maids in formation behind, waiting for the introductory organ music.

At the precise moment that they moved forward on cue, a gust of wind blew all the dresses straight up in the air above waist height! What a photo! Still gripping my camera after the last shot, I raised it to take the picture of a lifetime. I mentally phoned the local paper, and most of the dailies as I pressed the shutter release, disaster, nothing happened! Empty, devoid of film, no shots left!

I cursed my earlier enthusiasm with the bridesmaids' poses, and realised on later examination in the vestry at the register signing that I had wrongly loaded a twenty-four exposure film, not a thirty-six as supposed, which would undoubtedly have saved the day.

The moment was deliciously added to, however, by the young pageboy, George, who shouted out in a strident Cockney accent, "Cor! All their knickers are the same colour as their dresses, LOOK!"

Seven very red-faced ladies entered the church and I doubted if anyone inside had heard anything untoward outside as had we, and the rest of the wedding went off splendidly, both the group shots outside after the ceremony and at the reception nearby.

No mention was ever made of the 'Shot That Got Away', and in later years I was invited to do the weddings of four of the original girls, but no situation ever presented itself again! But – I live in hope!

Chapter 13
Tips

There was an aspect of cabbing that was never mentioned to the customer directly, discussed avidly among the other drivers when back at the office, and although not actually expected, gratefully received when offered. This may take the form of the most extraordinary objects, currencies and even verbal gifts. What is this mystery item? The TIP!

Many and wonderful have been the tips given to me over the years, and again a complete list would fill several pages even if I could remember them all accurately, so I have tried to set down the more memorable ones for you.

We regularly ferried a middle-aged lady from her house to the riding stables of her daughter, with whom she spent several nights a week, and she was quite generous money-wise. But after a particularly arduous journey's end spent rearranging some stable items that her daughter was supposed to have done, she turned to me and breathlessly asked me to accept a 'small gift', which I looked forward to, to accompany a well-earned cup of tea!

She led me outside and pointed proudly to a large pile of horse droppings.

"There is a sack in the corner," she prompted. "Grab a shovel and help yourself!"

Somewhat reluctantly I did so, and loaded the heavy, squashy sack into my boot. I left it outside, in a dark corner of the basement area of our flat, and there it stayed for several months, until the other residents begged me to either use it on the back garden or dump it somewhere else!

The boot, too, never did recover and always had a background fragrance of the countryside! (It went into a skip one dark night and vanished!)

Amateur, and sometimes professional punters would surreptitiously slip written tips for horse and dog races into my hand at the end of a journey with a promise from me not to share the animal's name with anyone else. (A large percentage of them did not bear any profit even when shared with the local bookmaker, who was always glad to see me in his shop!

A jovial local bon viveur hired me one day to take him to a town about ten miles away to pay a debt to a friend, and we duly set off. He had the same Christian name as myself, and we got on very well.

The friend was out, so Terry suggested stopping off on the way back home for a meal, on him. I agreed and we sat at a nearby pub. He could never hold his drink, and after several large ones, ate his meal then prepared to doze off, prevented only by my insistence that we left!

I saw him to his home and was astonished to be offered fifty pounds! He remembered nothing of this the next day, and seemed to show no remorse at spending vast amounts of money on the demon drink, so it was with great surprise that I presented him with the large banknote. Honesty does pay, and he told me to keep it with his thanks!

Another lovely customer, or so it seemed, was the Arab man who commuted regularly from his home in town to the Further Education College a few miles away. He was very keen on extending his command of the English language and computing, the more to further his own career in Dubai. He also went home frequently to his wife, and I took him to the airport several times both ways.

On the day of his graduation, and therefore the last day of his stay here, he asked to me to take him to catch a plane the following day, in the company of his wife, who had travelled over specially for the ceremony.

Much thought had gone into this, on his part, for on arrival at Heathrow, and after a genuinely sad farewell, I was gravely presented with a large, rigid pizza-type box, heavy and well-wrapped in a large carrier bag.

All the way back I puzzled just what this exciting package would be: a gold-rimmed wall plaque, a silver dish? I could only hurry home to find out.

I parked the car, hurried indoors, and finally opened the gift box. Guess what? It was a huge rice cake, solid and completely inedible!

Small gifts were frequently and gratefully offered and received; a piece of shopping like a cake, can of beer, and such things as a cat lover like myself might appreciate: a tin of cat food etc. but I think for sheer originality the prize for the most imaginative tip must go to the dear old soul, Mrs King.

She was a very regular churchgoer, a pillar in the local WI circles, an enthusiastic organiser of jumble sales for any reason whatsoever, and a thoroughly amiable person, a pleasure to take on her little rounds, so it was with a smile on my lips that I called on her one morning.

"I really don't know what to do," she told me at the door of her near little bungalow. "All this stuff has to be moved to the church hall by this afternoon. Do you think that two trips will be enough, for the committee only gave me five pounds for the transfer of all this lot?"

I looked at the piles of items on the floor, destined to be sold as jumble. I told her I would get as much as possible in, and loaded the cab accordingly. Two trips almost did the trick, but sadly left on her hall floor was an old oak draw-leaf table, huge and solid-looking. A friend had dumped it there, she said, more with relief than hope for sale!

"I really don't know what to do with this horrible thing," she told me. "I wonder if you could get rid of it for me, they won't pay for another trip, and I can't see this selling. People are throwing these tables away, aren't they?"

Now, dear reader you may like to know that it was not long since my wedding; money was tight, furniture was nearly non-existent, and our dining room table consisted of trays on our laps!

"I'll take it," I said eagerly. "I'll even make a contribution to your funds."

She clasped her hands into mind delightedly. "Oh I wish you would accept it as a gift," she said delightedly. "I know you are short of furniture, and this will last until you have saved up for something better; it must be over fifty years old already!"

I studied the object more closely, and it was indeed showing signs of many years of usage, but extremely solidly made, opening out to an impressive size with the pull-out leaves.

It was badly in need of sanding down and re-varnishing, but these jobs were no problem. I accept delightedly, and with great difficulty and the aid of her next door neighbour, we loaded the item into my cab, which it completely filled.

Back home, my wife was amazed and as pleased as me when we had unloaded it, and sited it in the dining room, where after some loving care had been lavished. It was used daily for over twenty years, then passed on to an equally broke and just married friend, where it still resides in its glory.

I never again received such an unusual but useful item, truly the King of Tips!

Chapter 14
Airports

Modern airports are essential parts of modern travel. To hurtle across to the other side of the world in as short a time as possible seems to be the norm now. Huge areas like Heathrow, with a choice of four departure points, soon to be even bigger with the opening of Terminal Five, are bewildering to the unwary traveller, and even more so to the rookie cab driver, but these throbbing, vibrant spaces can still provide laughs and tears in equal quantities to the budding author willing to jot down the stories as they happen!

In the sixties and seventies, Stansted was minute, just really an idea for a departure point, and Gatwick was still relatively small and friendly. Heathrow was then, as now, the BIG one, and while I never had enough time to get out and have a really good look around, the excitement of my passengers was usually transmitted to me, as I dropped them off with their mountains of luggage, or picked them up upon their return from exotic and far-flung places. Some people were lucky just to fly at all!

Such an occasion starred Yolande, a very pretty, but forgetful Italian student going back home to a tiny village after two weeks spent (quite uselessly) learning English in a local language school.

Mummy, in Italy, had forwarded enough money for her daughter's taxi fare, and yours truly was delegated to take her to the nearest airport, very early one winter's morning.

She obviously felt the cold as she resembled an Egyptian mummy, heavily swathed in several pullovers and thick coats. The moment that she had climbed into the cab was the signal for her to:

a) Burst into tears
b) Start peeling off layers of superfluous clothing, and,
c) Start to shout, and continue to shout for the entire length of the journey: "GAT-A-WICK! GAT-A-WICK! GAT-A-WICK!"

After a very few miles had gone by, I had had enough of this, as you can imagine, but nothing I could say would stem either the tears or the monotonous wailing.

I tried to converse with her but to no avail, and it was not until we swung into the departure drop-off point that I (jokingly, so I thought!) asked her if she had remembered her passport. Frantic fumbling into the interior of her garments, now re-donned, produced nothing. I had the horrible feeling that she had left it behind at her host family's house, and a phone call to my office to check this idea revealed the truth. It was there, all right, the first question was: what to do?

The office was not prepared to sanction the sending of another car to pick up the missing passport without pay, so a phone call to Mummy was contracted with some difficulty via the language school, and the money was promised, so it was with great relief that I welcomed the second driver on his arrival at Gatwick to meet us in the car park!

Fatigue had mercifully overtaken Yolande by this time so we woke her up to the happy news that she could at last travel out. She vanished inside, crying!

We travelled back to the office together, the passport deliverer and myself, and it was not the last time that that the happy traveller was made unhappy by their own forgetfulness, but I do really remember dear Yolande as most definitely the very NOISIEST!

Five quite major language schools resided in my hometown and many and varied were the students that we carried around of all ages. Most were polite and courteous, loving their first visit to a foreign country, and so were eager to converse with our drivers at every opportunity.

I had a few words of French from my days at school, and even fewer words of German gleaned from a solitary visit to Munster as a teenager. Russian, however, has remained a total mystery to this day, so it was probably Sod's law that dictated that the most amount of trouble with a student that I ever encountered, was with a young Russian called, yes, Ivan!

From an obviously wealthy family, he splashed money around with gay abandon, treating other students to taxi rides to and from his host family. This would have been an admirable trait had it not been for the fact that not only did he never seemingly have a note smaller than a twenty, especially first thing in the morning when my change was always at its lowest, but whenever time was at its shortest, which was most of the time in the early hours, he would lengthen his journey at the last minute to pick up several additional, unbooked passengers, which invariably made me late for the following job.

He was about thirteen years old, and streetwise beyond his years, but if I had my way, about to meet his match!

My chance came at the very end of his two weeks' stay, when he booked my firm to take him to the airport to leave at five in the morning. Guess who?

He was only just awake when I loaded his luggage in, and promptly fell asleep the moment he sat down. So it was a quiet journey, the only friendly sound being my constant companion: the radio permanently tuned to Radio Two.

I rehearsed my plan as we sped along, and implemented it as we turned in!

"Here we are," I said heartily. "Gatwick Airport, let's get your stuff out!"

He gazed blearily out of the window at the building, and shouted out as he read the large illuminated sign, proudly shining its name 'Heathrow'. "This is the wrong place!" he cried in dismay. "I told you Gatwick!"

"You said Heathrow," I exclaimed in mock horror, enjoying the moment.

"Gatwick!"

"Heathrow!"

"Gatwick!"

"Heathrow!"

I could not keep this up for much longer, so told him he WAS right, which calmed him down and he saw the joke as I unloaded his luggage.

"I did mess you about a bit, didn't I?" he admitted. "You did well to make your own joke onto me." He shook my hand and we were even, but then came a surprise that even my sense of humour could not have dreamed up. As an afterthought, he turned back from his loaded trolley, and added, "I have bought my father a present from England, would you like to see if he will like it?"

He rummaged in his bag and proudly withdrew a replica metal revolver!

"For goodness sake, don't wave that around!" I pleaded. "Put the thing back into your bag."

He gazed sadly at me and my reaction. "You DO think he will like it, don't you? It cost a lot of money from a shop in London, and the man said it was just like a real one!"

I stared at him is disbelief. Was he really going to try to take the gun in through security? The situation was priceless, and I cursed the fact that I could not go in with him to watch the fun, but we were only allowed literally five minutes to unload and go, so the end result was anybody's guess.

Ivan may well have gained a good working knowledge of English, but he was sadly lacking in old-fashioned common sense!

An idea struck him as he walked into the terminal. "I know," he shouted excitedly, "I'll show the policeman here!"

The end of my tale is sadly unknown, as I drove away chuckling, perhaps a shade cruelly. I tried to imagine the reaction of the constable inside. Perhaps Ivan is still there, I don't know, but for a long time afterwards, every trip to either airport brought back memories of the Russian lad and his gun! Strangely, the most popular souvenirs that were taken back to their homeland by the young Russians turned out to be bananas, and Easter eggs! I saw many of these, but never another revolver!

Chapter 15
Curry

We are available to carry MOST things, albeit at our discretion, but generally there is not much in the way of cargo that we will not touch, as long as it is legal, of course!

The Great Computer Day sticks in my memory as one bizarre example. I was to go to an industrial estate just outside town, my boss informed me. There my cab would be loaded with boxes of computers. My destination would be revealed when I was ready to leave. Intriguing, I thought, and ever-ready for pastures new, hurried off to the unit in question.

My first impression was that there was no way that all those large boxes would ever fit inside the taxi! Two fairly strong chaps helping me did eventually prove me wrong, but it WAS a very tight squeeze. I signed for them, then asked the man in charge where to deliver my expensive load.

"Oh, that's the easy part," he laughed, "go up the M25 until you reach the bridge over the road at junction twelve. You will meet our man there at midday, and he will take them from you into his van. It's bigger than this," he said contemptuously, "and probably a lot faster, because they have to be in Scotland by midnight. Off you go!" he added dismissively, and walked away, leaving me scribbling the instructions on the back of my hand!

Traffic was heavy on the motorway, and I had to hurry to meet the deadline, but eventually the said bridge hove into view, so I drove onto it to keep my mysterious appointment. I felt like some king of spy. Perhaps these computers were bugged, perhaps they contained vital State secrets, who could tell? Only the recipient at the final destination!

Now, actually parking in this area was hazardous, both from the point of view of car zooming past at a fairly high rate of knots, but also what could I possibly say to a traffic policeman if one showed up?

I had not been there more than ten fear-filled minutes, when a large white van pulled up alongside, the door sliding open before it had completely halted, and three men jumped out. They nodded at me, and as I opened MY doors they expertly and effortlessly transferred the boxes to their van, and though they were very deft and gentle, they kept up a constant all-round observation. The whole operation took no more than three or four minutes, and as they shut themselves in once more, one of them thrust an envelope into my hand, shouted, "Cheers, mate, you've saved our lives, bye!"

I ran over the events in my mind as I stared after them in amazement, then still in a daze, left the scene as quickly as the others.

The envelope, which I opened as soon as I had put some miles from the bridge, contained fifty pounds, a nice addition to the price paid to me by my boss for the journey, but who these men were and just what the cargo's destination and purpose were, I never found out, only that a few weeks later in the national press, a report was printed giving the story that 'several specially built computers, reputed to originate from a small factory somewhere on the South Coast had played a vital part in the arrest of members of an international smuggling ring'!

I was told no more, and so was it mere coincidence that my boss looked very smug for the rest of that week!

Equally bizarre, but much more messy was the WRVS Curry Run! This was beautifully organised, magnificently thought out, and disastrously executed by me!

The local Women's' Institute did a sterling job looking after, amongst other things, the elderly people that relied on them to provide a substantial hot meal in the local meeting hall and the SOS came through to us one summer's morning: a crisis was looming on the near horizon!

"The damn kitchen's let us down badly," said the harassed voice on the phone. "It needs completely making over immediately so we need one of your cabs to pick up the hot food from the usual caterers and deliver it down here to the hall. Can you oblige?"

Now, it happened that an elderly aunt of the boss was a daily visitor to the centre, and constantly raved about the quality and content of the food served there, so the outcome was a foregone conclusion!

The conveying of the containers was to last one week, the length of time that the decorators would hopefully take to render the place habitable again, and at first the plan went perfectly.

I would drive up to the caterers, load the sealed and piping hot containers into the luggage space of the cab, then run these down to the hall, there to be immediately opened and served to the ever-hungry members and the menus WERE good.

Hearty stews, tasty casseroles, and wholesome hotpots were all dished out and consumed with the customary relish, but the weekly winning favourite by a very long way was curry, ousting the previous number one, fish, by a clear majority. So Friday was madras day, and eagerly anticipated, indeed attendance was regularly up by a third on these occasions! (I did try it once, and it WAS good, that cook really knew his or her stuff!)

The loading took place as usual, but the girl that helped me this particular morning was new, and obviously not used to double-checking the tight seal of the containers lids! We both assumed the other had done this!

A disaster was imminent, but of course you don't see it until it's too late, do you? The loading continued, and was soon accomplished on time.

As I set off as usual, heavily laden, the all-pervading aroma of curry that normally disappeared as soon as I had turned the first corner still lingered! I stole a look in my rear view mirror at the fragrant cargo and froze!

Three of the lids had slipped off their containers and the hot meaty contents were merrily slopping backwards and forwards, spreading themselves over the entire back floor area, adding a pungency that hitherto I would not have believed possible in the enclosed environment of my previously spotless cab's interior! Something would have to be done, and urgently!

The journey was not a long one, and I could not do much else other than to continue, trying desperately to find the straightest, smoothest lengths of road. (Our council did not spend much on road maintenance!)

When I DID arrive and opened the rear doors to assess the damage done, the resultant mess was incredible, not to mention the aroma!

A thick layer of best madras curry ebbed and flowed gently across the fitted rubber floor mat, which matched exactly the coating on the seats, where the odd containers that could not be accommodated on the floor usually happily resided! This was going to take SOME clearing up!

My misery did not end there, because as I lifted out the first swiftly-wiped container, and walked into the eating areas of the centre, the lady in charge met me halfway across the floor, shaking her head at me.

"Didn't you get our phone call?" she anxiously asked, "WE cancelled this delivery early this morning!" She hurried away disinterestedly.

To say that I was very annoyed was the understatement of the week. I manhandled the vessel back out to the car, placed it back on the curried floor, then rang my boss, my cab radio being out of range here.

"Oh yes," he said matter-of-factly, "we've been trying to contact you, but the radio's down here in the office. We will charge them anyway, so just return to base."

After I had put him in the picture he arranged for a local valeting firm to meet me for the big clean up, and they made a fantastic job of it, but for a very, VERY long time afterwards, I made doubly sure that the lids WERE properly fitted and many were the passengers that pointedly sniffed at the lingering aroma at the moment of getting in.

Perhaps they assumed I lived on curry, I don't know, but I would have loved shares in air-fresheners!

Chapter 16
Gamblers

"Bloody trains!"

"Yeah, bloody trains!"

An overnight sprinkling of snow, probably the 'wrong' sort, had made a nonsense of British Rail's schedule for the morning at least, so several disgruntled passengers had migrated from the platform to our warmer office next door, each one protesting loudly to anyone who would listen about the poor service, being late for work, having missed appointments, etc.

The two large red-faced men who had just spoken had elbowed their way to the front of the queue, and were belligerently demanding a taxi as soon as possible, if not sooner. Their destination, as yet, undisclosed.

As we operated a first in, first out, rota, it was my fare.

The controller caught my eye, and I walked out to them from the drivers' room to the waiting area. "Plumpton Racecourse," said one man. "I presume you know the way, and we have to be there in under one hour, and thirty-five quid is scandalous, but we have no choice. So COME ON!"

The accent was North Country, but the tone was not friendly. I did not know the way, never having been to the racecourse itself, but I knew that the route led through Lewes, the nearest town, and one hour was pushing their luck considering the conditions. I said so, quickly setting my Sat nav.

"You won't need that gizmo," said the same man. "I know every inch of the way. I've been there dozens of times in my Jag, which is more comfortable that this heap, so get a move on!"

The obvious leader of the two squeezed in behind me as I mentally groaned at his statement. I had heard this many times before, and a few people DID direct me accurately, but they were VERY few in number. His partner heaved their travelling bags onto their laps, and I pulled out of the yard to the delighted looks of the remaining drivers, who, to a man, revelled in the misfortunes of others!

While my disgruntled pair were noisily and unhappily settling themselves in the back, I wondered how much snow had fallen in the Lewes area, as it was reported to be thicker inland. These two would not tolerate further delays, but the nightmare journey was only just beginning, as I soon found out!

The roads were mainly clear, although the verges had a thin covering of discoloured snowy slush, and it was clear that the surrounding high ground had been covered completely, though a watery sun was trying to break through the gloomy sky.

A short tunnel led into the outskirts of the town, and I confidentially turned left as we exited.

A sharp finger prodded me between the shoulder blades. "Wrong way!" he growled. "I thought you said you knew the way?"

I sighed. Here we go, I thought, and pulled out to put my case to him. "The Sat Nav is leading us by the most direct route through the town." I started to say. "And…"

"Rubbish!" said the same impatient voice. "Turn that wretched contraption off. I've found my way through here dozens of times, now I'll show you the correct route!"

I looked at him in my mirror, and he was smirking knowingly at his companion. I couldn't win this one. I paused my direction finder, but did not turn it fully off, just in case!

I gathered from the unhappy conversation they had along the way, that this was a regular event for one of them but the other was going for the first time. Refreshments were laid on at the course, but only up until a certain time, which had now elapsed, hence the previous urgency. If we were quick enough they would still make the first race, but it would be close, very close.

"Right, come on," he started. "Turn left, up the hill, then right at the top, come on, come on!"

We pulled off and I did as directed, only to find a large, new dustcart blocking our way. Exclamations of annoyance came instantly from the back seat, but we just had to sit there. As we slid past after what seemed ages, more directions followed.

"Down the hill, then left at the bottom, that leads you straight onto to the Plumpton road. I dunno, call yourself a cabbie!"

We went down the hill, turned left, and carried on by the only exit available, BACK THROUGH THE TUNNEL!

"You obviously can't follow even the most basic instructions, can you!" ranted my guide. "Now turn around and do as I said!"

I did so, and we were back at the tunnel again in no time!

We did this once more, and by now the novelty was wearing off, so I restarted the Sat nav. I deliberately turned up the volume and following the verbal directions, soon rejoined the proper road out of town. I even soon picked out a 'To the Racecourse' sign. Within four miles we would be there. My advisor now sat in silence, apart from one remark that 'they' had probably changed the town centre since he had come this way the last time.

Their free lunch was now over, and therefore, horror of horrors, they would have to buy some, and did I know how much it cost on course?

The snow had been thicker on this climb out of town, and the surrounding high ground looked like the Alps. I wondered if the racing was still on, and said so, but judging by the number of race goers vehicles in the car park as we entered, it was.

I soon realised that I had wrongly come into the 'Members Enclosure', but by now I was past caring and ready to use the "Oh, sorry, I've never been here before, isn't this right then?" ploy, but no one challenged me, just a cursory glance from a burly steward, who had probably seen lost drivers many times before.

I found a space, and pulled in, with a look at my watch. What SHOULD have taken, as the man said about one hour, had taken nearly two, but the sun was now shining brightly, and I was really going to enjoy my solitary ride back.

With great relief, I let the two punters out, was grudgingly paid the EXACT fare, and watched as I drove straight back out, as they scuttled off to the nearest marquee. Probably the beer tent, I though longingly.

I stopped just up the road for a muchly-needed cigarette and for some reason opened my paper at the racing page. The name of a horse leaped out at me from that morning's list: 'Northern Navigator'!

Should I push my luck and have a flutter? Nah, I'd had enough, and retracted my steps back to the office, and recounted my tale to the eagerly awaiting drivers, who received it with great glee.

The horse? Ah, yes, I checked the results in the paper the next morning. Not a mention, a loser, just like my two 'gents'!

Chapter 17
Snow

The very next day, another customer was similarly stranded and was cursing the non-appearance of the train, and the non-disappearance of the snow, which although not too much of a problem locally for us to navigate around the worst affected streets, did not help those who had to get out of town.

The pleadings of this passenger were heard in our inner rest room, and I could tell by the unanimous shaking of heads that no one was prepared to undertake the journey to a town about twenty miles away, however, urgent the cause might be. The morning had been a slow one, so I walked out into the reception area and studied the stricken gent.

He was in obvious distress, a little suited middle-aged figure, and he turned an anguished face to me, shrugged his shoulders and said, "Well, if you aren't prepared to risk it, I understand. Now I really don't know what to do. I suppose I could try the police station."

He walked dejectedly outside and stood looking forlornly at the thin covering of snow on the road, sighing deeply.

"What is his problem?" I asked the controller. Apparently he had stayed in a hotel overnight for a meeting and had to cut the two-day arrangement short because his pedigree dog had been injured in the icy conditions back home, so he was most anxious to get there by any means possible. His wife anxiously awaited the vet.

As a compulsive animal lover, I couldn't leave him here. "Come on," I called over my shoulder at him, as I got into my cab, fired it up and set the wipers to clear the thin film on the windscreen. "I'll take you as far as I can, BUT," I turned to face him as he scrambled gratefully into the back, "if it's too bad, I'll drop you where it's safe for both of us, OK?"

He eagerly accepted to this, and after the fare was accepted, he offered me a generous tip on top when we got there.

We set off, the main roads quite acceptable, but the flakes got bigger after about fifteen miles, the surrounding countryside well covered, so it was with considerable relief that we turned off the main road into a side road that AT FIRST looked reasonably navigable, at least at the top!

I had been given an uninterrupted talk about the Labrador he owned and was obviously enamoured with, the life history, illnesses, and so on, but I had to cut off his verbal flow to allow me to concentrate on the slalom ahead. This 'road' was a beauty! The level, snow-covered track, for that's what it had rapidly degenerated into, began to slope downhill, so I applied the handbrake and slid gently to a stop.

"This is splendid," he enthused. "I can walk these last few yards, thank you so much." He settled up with me, I wished him luck with the injured animal, then the landscape seemed to literally swallow him, for I saw no opening for a house.

The snow continued to fall, if anything heavier, and it was definitely getting a lot colder. I restarted, and tried to gently reverse to go back to the main road, but I rapidly found to my horror and consternation that, practically, I could only move forward; the slope was too much to get purchase, so I had no choice but to go gingerly further down and hope the lane either flattened out, or changed direction to my advantage. To make things worse, I was dying for a pee! This on my own would not be a problem, for the area was deserted, but I dared not leave the cab parked while I used the nearest bush, for fear of it slithering downhill empty.

The further I went down, the steeper the angle; there was no end to the track. I slithered to a stop in a shallow ditch and considered my options. Call a breakdown service, try again somewhere to turn around and attempt to backtrack, or – well that was as far as I had got to when I heard a voice outside. I opened my window to see a diminutive figure smiling toothlessly at me. He wore a ancient, threadbare coat, open at the neck, and seemed impervious to the elements.

"I'll bet you're stuck. You're not local, otherwise you wouldn't even have tried to come down here and you need my loo. Am I right?" He gleefully looked up at me, and I could only smile back at him and nod my head in agreement.

At least I was not stuck AND alone.

"Thought so," he continued gleefully. "Leave your cab there, and I'll sort you out. Come on, follow me!" He went through a gap in the hedge I hadn't noticed and led me over the snow-covered grass and into a large barn, floored with straw, and smelling strongly of horses. The warmth inside was really welcome, and I said so.

"There's a bucket in the corner, you can pee in there," he gestured vaguely. "I'll make you a cuppa then get the tractor out."

By the time I had attended to my most urgent needs, he had returned with a steaming cup each. What nectar! We chatted briefly. He was used to stricken vehicles, and told me that the lane degenerated further down into a swampy area, and that it was dead end too. He had, he continued, just come out for a last look around before retiring, as he was up early, and closed up early. He managed a smallholding, but winter severely cut his work down. There were just two barns, he said and the fields.

"I'll get the tractor out, you'll be back on the main road in no time, finish your tea. I'll only be a jiffy."

He chuckled to himself and walked out of the barn, only to walk straight back in, carrying a coil of rope and leading by the reins a huge shire horse. The animal stood placidly and regarded me with complete indifference. I barely reached his shoulder and he radiated power. He munched something contentedly.

So this was the 'tractor' he mentioned. He threaded the rope expertly through the horse's bridle, led it outside, and bade me fix the ends to my rear bumper. I complied still in disbelief.

"You get back in and steer," he told me, and proceeded to walk the huge animal back up the tract. The rope tightened and as the cab moved steadily backwards, I could feel the enormous power of the horse steadily pulling. The weight of the cab seemed to be almost of no consequence, and soon, as promised, we emerged onto the welcome and gloriously gritted main highway.

He unhitched my benevolent creature, who seemed quite unfazed by the whole journey. And turned its head to return home.

My saviour steadfastly refused any payment for their services, but as I shook his hand in thanks, my palm returned empty of the note I had palmed. It was well worth it, what a lovely man and beast.

I got back to base a little later than anybody expected, including me. I called it a day and thankfully returned home to eat and rest.

The dog owner phoned his thanks the next day to our office. The vet had been in attendance, the dog bandaged and in no danger. I thought it best not to mention my benefactor's rescue of me, and of course, after a couple more days, the snow had mostly gone.

In the spring, by coincidence, I had to journey again to the same town, so made a short detour down that wretched lane. I found the barn, still with the lovely horse 'tractor', and sought out the old chap.

He still had the cheery, toothless infectious grin, and of course remembered me. I guessed his liking for a drink, and presented him with a bottle of a good single malt. One good turn, etc. A lovely man.

Chapter 18
Telethon

Companies came and went, as did cars and bosses, but the basic jobs remained the same, with thankfully interesting interludes in between to liven up the days, which could get a bit boring.

Time accelerated alarmingly, and it was now the occasion for the Telethon, the modern version of which is named Children In Need. The basic idea was to raise as much money as possible, in as many crazy ways as possible, for children's' charities.

These collections, with the collectors involved, would then appear in front of an audience at the nearest TV studios to present their contributions, usually in the form of a giant cheque, provided by (and probably overcharged for the privilege by) the appropriate bank. An evening long programme, with live broadcasts from the various regions promised to be entertaining. Celebrities were encouraged to attend, and the broadcasts were widely advertised in the press and on TV. The nation's interest was aroused and people were ready to partake.

Many weird and wacky events were formulated and announced in the week preceding the event, and it occurred to me in an idle moment that we, too, could participate. The other drivers had been replaced as they flowed in and out of the firm, but the majority of the remaining lads were as quirky and sometimes downright daft as myself! Well, almost.

Suggestions were mulled over, but most were rejected as being too rude, too risky, or downright illegal. As the big event day was fast approaching, we just had to find an idea that other taxi firms in the town had not thought of, for by now there were quite a few setting up operations, ranging from drivers dressing as women, setting a standard fare for any area of town with a pound from each trip going into the pot, to handing out badges that were also sold for a pound, again to swell the charity takings. Novelty was paramount, something that the other firms had not yet arranged.

The next day I had it, the BIG IDEA! There were several drivers in the ops room, when I burst in, including our boss.

"I've got it! I cried. "We'll PULL the cab from one end of the seafront to the other with ropes and the others can follow us with buckets to collect the cash from the shops and pubs."

There was dead silence, following quickly by unanimous laughter, some of them miming my idea, doubling over in mirth.

I warmed to my theme. "Think of it," I continued, "our boss can have T-shirts printed with the firm's name on so that the contributors can see where we're coming from, and he can get some plastic buckers with the firm's name on like a sticker."

The lads still showed doubtful expressions now that the initial amusement had died down, so it was time to play my ace!

"You really don't get the big picture, do you?" I continued. "The people who have invented the most original ways of collecting the money will be invited to the TV studios to present the final sum in front of the mega-famous celebrities. They will be interviewed by the broadcaster, with the method by which the collection was done. If our taxi, with appropriate door stickers (which we can't remove without the say so of our council) was invited too, in front of cameras, just think of the FREE PUBLICITY! The drivers' wives and girlfriends could do the collecting, with any off duty drivers."

There was dead silence, then everybody started talking at once. The rest of the day passed in making plans for the big day the following week. Our boss never mucked about when HE thought he had a good idea! A skeleton staff was arranged to give our customers the best service with the cars left, and Sunday dawned.

The cab was taken off the road, serviced, washed and polished within an inch of its life and re-stickered. It looked like a showroom vehicle, and when the council official came round to give his official permission and blessing, all was ready.

Monday morning saw the gleaming cab with its volunteer driver ensconced. He had strict instructions not to exceed ten miles an hour when the cab was under power, but for the main drag it would be pulled in neutral. Plastic buckets were dished out. When hopefully filled, they would be emptied into a plastic dustbin inside the cab, relocking the doors as it proceeded.

The same councillor was to officially see us off, and the local paper sent a keen young photo-journalist. All was ready. At precisely nine o'clock, on this gorgeous sunny day, the flag went up, then down, cameras flashed by the small but enthusiastic band of well-wishers, the journalist leaped along the pavement to get a head-on shot. Two brawny lads in the road heaved on one rope each, the cab's wheels turned once, then a rope snapped!

It seemed, in the post mortem afterwards, that these were obtained from the local fish market, judging by the strong smell of fish and tar on the hands of the pullers. They were free, but rotten.

Newer replacements were sent for a refitted, and at last the fundraiser got underway. We, the collectors, fanned out and targeted every café, pub and boarding house within easy reach. Once we announced the cause, most people contributed generously and by the time we had reached approximately the halfway mark, the coins and not a few notes were pouring into the dustbin quite satisfactorily. Well, until they got the puncture!

A large piece of broken bottle glass had again scuppered out attempt. We could see some sort of a problem had occurred, as we had forged ahead on foot, but the cab was stopped. Normally the spare wheel could be put on in a matter of minutes, especially with all the extra hands available, but it only took a look in the boot to fine no spare! Dire threats were issued against the perpetrator. (The same rope provider had also removed the spare to pump up the slightly soft tyre at his house, and it was still there!)

A passing, (though rival) cab driver was persuaded to donate his spare just for a couple of hours, and we were off again, this time to finish in a pub car park at the end of the seafront, hot and bothered, but triumphant in our good deed done.

Shandies on the boss, and we heartily congratulated each other with lots of photos taken and promises of almost everlasting fame by the paper. Still waiting.

The dustbin was unloaded, the contents taken away for counting, and the next day earmarked for our TV debut. T-shirts were washed and ironed, hairdos done, optimism reigned, for now.

Countless video timers were set for the following evening, the cab was again valeted and we were all hard at work fixing loads of balloons to the car door handles and every wheel, again with our name and phone number printed on, early the next morning.

We could carry five passengers only, so the rest of the joyful rabble went in their own cars, as excited as kids, like us. Our boss announced a total of over seven hundred pounds. It had taken, he said, more than four hours to count, helped by his wife. It would have to be an ordinary cheque, as time was short.

We set off, to the great hilarity of the other drivers who passed us. Upon arrival the parking attendant at the studio had strict orders NOT to admit any vehicles past the visitors' area, so that was the first real disappointment. But at least we had made it here.

We were shown to the audience area, seated, and watched enthralled as the announcer moved amongst the people waving large cheques, stopping here and there to enquire where they were from and how they had collected the cash. He moved closer, our moment had come, our boss rose to his feet smiling in anticipation, the rest of us showing off out T-shirts to the camera.

"And here is the taxi-pulling team from the seaside," he announced, "with seven hundred pounds to give us!" He moved so swiftly on that we were left wondering if that was out moment of glory. It was!

The video tapes played back when we got back home lasted twenty-two seconds! (Some said twenty-three, but I think they exaggerated!)

We stayed for a couple more hours, then drove back, balloons dwindling rapidly.

No celebrities were even glimpsed, although I did stand next to Brian Cant in the gents! Still, a really good day out.

Would we do it all again? Oh, yes, but perhaps with a new idea!

Chapter 19
Karate

I wonder how many times during the course of a week we hear the expressions: You'll be the death of me, I wouldn't be seen dead in that, in the dead of night, I'm deadly serious' etc, and probably dozens more. You would hope they did not apply to someone in a journey by cab, until it actually happened, preferably to someone else.

Well, it did happen to somebody one day – me!

Alan came down from London one summer to retire from the stresses from living in a huge city. He fancied the seaside. After looking for some time at flats to rent, he settled on buying a large static caravan, in a big site just off the seafront and set about making it home.

Garden centres were easily found within a twenty-minute ride and were duly visited, their stock perused and selections made. He had found our number in the office of the site, and used us regularly and enthusiastically. All our drivers liked him; he used to like us to help him plant out the periphery of his little homemade garden. Within a few weeks it was as if it always had been there, and he was very proudly going to show his parents coming down from London to visit where he lived and how he had improved the area from a simple mud patch to a really useful collection of flowers, shrubs and herbs, especially the latter, for he loved to cook.

What was he like? Well, he studied martial arts, taking part in some quite important competitions, and judging by the rows of certificates, cups and medals he displayed on the walls and sideboard in his caravan, he was a competent and skilled fighter.

On one particularly slow afternoon, he invited me in to tea with him, and so opened the door into a fascinating insight of his life. Racks of ceremonial swords were evidently a favourite topic. Judo, Ai-kido, Ju Jitsu, he had worked his way thought most of the usual art forms, but it was not until I casually mentioned that I had briefly tried to learn the rudiments of Karate, and that my favourite action hero was Steven Seagal, that his eyes really lit up.

Now Alan was not tall, just average, and not thin either, perhaps a little overweight, but his gaze when he looked you straight in the eyes was sometimes a bit unnerving, and I could imagine him psyching out his opponent as they started their match.

He was, of course, always pleasant with us, but there was always a kind of background menace to him, although he told me his fighting days were long gone. Too many matches he said had injured him too many times. Broken bones were not unusual, with cuts, strained muscles and bruises being the normal outcome.

As I listened, I was rather glad that I had not continued MY training. (We thought naïvely that we would be out heroically defending ourselves within a week, but the reality was that eighteen months on, I had only reached the yellow belt stage. Family commitments and work pressure favoured a halt from the classes, so I left, thankfully injury free.)

He described to me with considerable relish some of his winning bouts, and he was particularly proud of one in which he stood toe to toe with his opponent. They could do literally anything they liked to each other, but the moment that the foot contact was broken, the person that had delivered the blow that caused it would be the winner. I could imagine it. I wouldn't like to watch.

He tended to move around quite painfully, sometimes complaining of arthritis, a badly aching knee, or a stiff shoulder or two. His age was probably around fifty, but his diet and lifestyle was not good. Alcohol and pizzas are OK in moderation, but…

His usual forays out usually started about nine or ten in the morning, so I was most surprised and not a little worried to answer the phone to him at six one morning.

"Pete," he croaked. I could hardly hear him. "Take me to the local A&E Department. I feel terrible. Please hurry!"

I reached his van within minutes, and rang the bell. No answer. Again. No answer. But in pressing my ear to the thin aluminium door, I could hear moaning. This was an emergency.

I turned the door handle and pushed with all my strength. It moved, and I could just see a leg behind it on the floor. I pushed again, and squashed myself through the gap onto the floor.

Alan lay full-length in front of me. He struggled to get himself up to a sitting position, but he was obviously too weak. His breathing sounded terrible, and it was all he could manage to grip my hand. I moved straight to the phone. "I'm calling an ambulance, Alan, stay down and try to keep calm." I am a first aider, and I'll stay here until the come."

"No," he mumbled. "No ambulance, you take me!"

I dropped the as yet undialled phone. I tried to change his mind, but he was adamant. It had to be me, and judging by his extreme breathlessness and red face, as soon as I could.

After what seemed an age, he could sit up, then stand, then weakly sink into a chair, but his condition was worrying me so much that I insisted he got into my cab parked literally two yards from his door.

A great deal of pushing, pulling huffing and puffing later, I belted him into the seat, hurriedly locked his van, then took off, not really caring at this still early time of the day whether or not there was some eager police car around some corner or my route! The reason for my extreme hurry would have been glaringly obvious!

His speech was better, though slurred, and I suspected a partial stroke. Within sight of the hospital, however, he slumped in his seat, his eyes closing. I shouted at him, but he didn't answer.

As I screeched into the A&E area, I shouted to an ambulance driver who had just pulled in. He took one look at the situation, then literally pulled Alan out onto a trolley with the aid of two more colleagues, and rushed him inside.

They would not let me in, so I carried on down to the police station to report it. They said they would let me know the outcome, but I doubted Alan survived.

They agreed that I had done the right thing in taking Alan myself, and I later learned that the ambulance team could not have saved him, had I called them. A massive heart attack, and a simultaneous, though smaller, stroke had done for him what countless opponents could not.

His parents called me the following week to hear the story, and thanked me for my diligence.

For weeks I went over the events. Could I have done more? My conscience was clear, but then so are my memories of a character the like of which you may only come across once.

I was thankful I had.

Chapter 20
Turf

If the final question in one of the contemporary quizzed on TV to win the big prize was: 'How many rolled up pieces of turf could you get in the back of a black cab, assuming each piece was one foot by three feet?' the averagely intelligent viewer would be extremely lucky to guess within a dozen and get anywhere near the correct answer. If you are ever asked, call me! Here's why.

Barry was not a fanatical gardener, he watched a few of the more popular how-to-grow-anything programmes the same as lots of viewers, and generally got the hang of most things in the end. He used us quite frequently, and blundered harmlessly through life. He dug, planted and harvested. He knew stuff, but not grass!

He had proudly supervised the design, construction and execution of an extensive patio in the rear garden of his modest bungalow, and had decided that a grassy surround would finish it off nicely. Crescent-shaped, modern and professionally laid.

That was the good news that he greeted me with as I drew up outside. His mission, and my job, was not immediately apparent, until he dug out a large tarpaulin from the shed and proceeded to line the floor and rear seating area of my cab. I protested.

"What on earth are you doing, Barry? I'm not shifting soil or rubbish in my vehicle, you'll have to get it carted down to the tip."

"Oh no, Pete," he answered, "it's only a load of turf to be returned to the garden centre. They've sent the wrong sort this morning. Before I could check it, the boke had upended the tipper, dropped the stuff down my sideway, stuck the delivery note in my letterbox and shot off down the street. I rang the centre, but they're so busy that they couldn't pick them up and re-deliver inside three days, and my mate is coming here later today to help me lay them. I must have them changed by then, and so I thought of you," he ended lamely.

I presumed it to be a compliment, and took it as such. You just could not like Barry. Not yet, anyway.

I walked down the sideway and what I saw did not fill me with enthusiasm. An untidy pile of green and green/brown rolls of turf had been unceremoniously dumped in an untidy pile. IF I agreed, WE would have to shift them between us. To make things worse, Barry then informed me that he could not come with me to help the changeover, as he had a dental appointment in one hour's time. Wonderful! I started to like him a bit less.

I would almost certainly regret agreeing to it, but I quoted him a price that would include waiting time, my labour, journeys there and back, and allowing also for the inevitable unforeseen hiccups that always, ALWAYS creep in.

We started loading, but not before I had donned an old long coat kept for mucky jobs like this one. The turves were not really heavy, just very moist, and a fair amount of earth adhered to the reverse. Three quarters of an hour later the cab's interior was nearly filled with some on the seats. Barry gave me the name of the correct type of grass, the delivery note, and after a quick cup of tea and cigarette, I drove off, panting slightly from my exertions.

A little voice told me this was not going to go according to our plan, but I subdued it. I should have listened.

Pulling up outside the centre, I hurried inside to explain. The manager was out, I was told by a young spotty lad behind the counter. He had been put in charge for a couple of hours, so how could help? He seemed keen, and I was pushed for time.

I carefully and slowly related my story, but he shook his head doubtfully. He went outside, I followed, still hopeful.

"See, I haven't got the authority to exchange goods. I just sell stuff from the shop and answer queries. Sorry," he ended lamely. "Mind you," he said proudly, "I can drive a forklift!"

This could be the answer I was seeking and formed THE PLAN!

"Right," I told him, "here's what I suggest. Put a sign on this door 'Closed for Lunch. Back in an hour', that sort of thing. We unload the wrong turves between us onto a pallet. You toddle off on your forklift, swap them over – you have enough of the correct sort, I hope?"

He nodded. I think I was getting through.

"Then," I continued, drawing a fiver out of my pocket and laying it on the counter right in front of him, "we reload my cab. I've got the correct grass, Barry and his mate can lay it today, your manager will be impressed, and you've gained this fiver."

The plan appealed to him, we did exactly that, and it was inside an hour that I was heading back to Barry. The new grass had just arrived and was even wetter, but still so far, so good. I was happy.

There was just enough rear window to see through in my mirror to catch a glimpse of the flashing blue light behind me, so I slowed to a crawl and pulled over. So did the police car. Wonderful!

I have always found that politeness helps in these cases, so I got out and approached the traffic patrol car, meeting the driver halfway along the pavement. He was young, unsmiling and keen.

"You've got a brake light out, sir," he opened. "Are you carrying?"

"Er, y-yes, officer," I stammered. "But not passengers."

He walked to the cab, opened the door and looked down in amazement as a thin trickle of muddy water poured gently onto his highly polished boots. A two-inch thick worm flopped onto one toecap and wriggled weakly. He looked at me aghast. I tried not to smile.

"I hope you haven't overloaded this vehicle, sir?" he continued, shaking off the invertebrate. "That would be unfortunate."

This had not occurred to me. Well I did not reckon on this intervention, so I said they HAD been weighed, I would get the bulb changed, and my destination was literally around the corner.

The officer's partner called him at that precise moment saying they had an urgent call, so he very reluctantly walked back, still shaking his boots.

Barry's turf-layer was waiting at the house. Barry was nursing a frozen jaw, and the unloading was still to come, but at least there was now three sets of hands to accomplish the task.

The easiest way to clean out my cab was by hose. We took out the tarpaulin and the fitted rubber floor mats, washed everything and repaired to the kitchen to tea and cigarettes.

I told Barry the police would probably ring him later, as I had told them the turves were stolen! He did not find this funny! (I did!)

An unusual interlude, probably it would never occur again, but it brightened up my day, and yes, I did get the offending bulb fixed.

Pardon? Oh, I forgot to tell you the number. One hundred and thirty-four, and they're HEAVY!

Conclusion

Over thirty years in the same job sounds like a very long time, and so it is, but the sheer variety of daily happenings has made the time pass extraordinarily quickly.
They still occur, so I will keep writing about them.
Book two is on the way!